Janet Fletcher was ordained in 2000 within the Church of England and is now Team Vicar in the Walton Team, Liverpool. A part of her ministry is spent at Liverpool Cathedral as Honorary Chaplain. She completed the Spiritual Accompaniment Courses for Prayer Guiding and also for Spiritual Direction at Loyola Hall, Rainhill, Prescot, a Jesuit Spirituality Centre. Janet's spirituality is formed through the Ignatian tradition, especially through the Nineteenth Annotation of the Ignatian Exercises, although Celtic Spirituality also finds a place within her spiritual thinking. Another dimension to her spiritual and prayer life comes from being a Tertiary member of the Order of the Holy Paraclete. She also enjoys leading quiet days and retreats, and the teaching of prayer and spirituality through study days or courses.

PATHWAY TO GOD

Following the Way in Prayer

Janet Fletcher

First published in Great Britain in 2006

Society for Promoting Christian Knowledge
36 Causton Street
London SW1P 4ST

Copyright © Janet Fletcher 2006

British Library Cataloguing-in-Publication Data
A catalogue record for this book is available from the British Library.

ISBN-13: 978–0–281–05818–1
ISBN-10: 0–281–05818–0

1 3 5 7 9 10 8 6 4 2

Typeset by Kenneth Burnley, Wirral, Cheshire
Printed in Great Britain by Ashford Colour Press

To all who share with me,
my own Pathway to God

Contents

Foreword

I've never met anyone who claimed to be an expert on prayer! It seems we are all novices. If you've picked up this book because you feel in need of help, then read on! Janet is a priest in the Diocese of Liverpool and has written this short yet helpful book out of her experience as a pastor, listening to the stories and struggles of those who try to pray. There's a spiritual instinct in us all: there's not a person who does not, at some stage in life, find the need to pray.

When the disciples said to Jesus, 'Lord, teach us to pray', I'm not sure if they realized that these words were themselves a prayer! It's not a bad place at which to begin; letting your heartfelt and truest thoughts come to the surface in a God-ward direction is the opening of the door. As you journey through the stages of this book under Janet's direction, this will be a good prayer with which to begin: 'Lord, teach me to pray'.

If you've got even this far in the Foreword, then it is a sign of a spiritual stirring and of the work of God's grace in your life. God made us to know and to love him. When we aspire to such, we are beginning to flourish as he intended. Knowing and loving God were the qualities that marked out Jesus – not that this made praying an easy experience for him. He sometimes sweated in prayer and often felt churned up inside. Prayer is not always serene.

In these pages, Janet takes the reader to Jesus, whose master-class in prayer led his first disciples to learn from him. But to go there to him is not simply to conjure up a figure from history. The New Testament transmits a vitally important message from eternity to every successive generation that Jesus, who prayed in the valley and on the mountain and in the garden and on the cross, is still praying to the good Father. And for us. To begin to pray is to enter into the conversation that is being had at this moment between the three persons of the Trinity. We will enter this circle of conversation with all the faltering, naïve and even precocious babbling of a toddler trying to join in the conversation of grown-up members of the family. But just as such infantile prattling will often meet with joy and laughter, so our prayers will meet with divine delight.

Rt Revd James Jones
Bishop of Liverpool

Preface

———◆———

This particular Pathway to God began its journey as a nine-week study course on prayer at St John's Church in Ainsdale, Southport, where I was curate. The aim of the course was to open up different ways of coming to God in prayer, and to look at how every prayer we pray develops and deepens our relationship with God. The next stage of the Pathway developed through articles written in 2005 for *Cathedral Life*, a monthly magazine published by and distributed at Liverpool Cathedral. Initially it was based on some of the themes covered in the course but it very quickly grew as other topics on prayer and spirituality were added. The Pathway has continued its route, and with this book there comes the most surprising and challenging stretch of its journey – and again much more has been included!

There are many books about prayer and spirituality. This one has found its way through the questions that I have been asked, as I have listened to people talk of their prayer life, and in particular wondering how to start – a seeking for the simple practicalities. *Pathway to God* is offered in the hope that it may provide a beginning, or a new dimension, on the journey towards a more intimate relationship with the God who always journeys with us; to open up the treasure trove of prayer and find for the first time, or again, some of the ways in which we can come to God in the wonder of our prayer.

We all need somewhere to start, and at times we also need an oasis to sit beside as we seek to refresh ourselves, and so discover once more the simplicity of a prayer that will lead us further along the Pathway towards a deeper and more profound encounter with God, who is our eternal travelling companion.

I believe that if we are to discover our spiritual home within the world that is our temporary home, then the Pathway between the two is prayer. By having the desire to meet with God in prayer, to be open to experiencing the Spirit's presence, and seeking to become more prayerful is the key to the door that brings us to life in faith, and enables us to live our lives through our very own personal experience of, and relationship with, God.

The Rublev Icon, by the Russian monk Andrei Rublev (*c.* 1370–1430), portrays the meeting of Abraham with the three strangers or angels at the oaks of Mamre (Genesis 18.1–5). The three angels are seen as representing the Trinity – Father, Son and Holy Spirit. The way the persons of the Trinity are seated in the icon looks as though they are *issuing the invitation* to come and join the circle of relationship. There is a space open and prepared for us. The decision to accept is ours to make. The invitation to journey along a Pathway of personal prayer is one of relationship with the Trinity, calling us to journey deeper into our selves, and so into the depths of God, in a way that will then send us back out into the world with a prayer that embraces more effectively the whole of creation.

Pathway to God is a personal journey of discovery of the inner self and of God. Yet the many different prayers to be prayed and experienced are offered in the hope that however personal they may at first appear, they will transform at the same time the prayer and the lives of faith offered, and given, to the wider communities to which we belong.

Each chapter flows into the one that follows, although each can also be read as a chapter on its own. At the end of each chapter there is a Pause for Prayer, and at the end of Chapters 8 and 9 there is also a Reflection. The prayers that are offered are prayers which reflect the theme of the chapter.

Preface

Although I am a member of the Tertiary Order of the Holy Paraclete, which is an Anglican Order, the background of my own spiritual life comes from the Ignatian tradition, of Ignatius of Loyola the founder of the Jesuits. Participating in the Nineteenth Annotation of the Ignatian Spiritual Exercises opened up a Pathway of prayer which led to a deeper awareness of the God who embraces the whole of my life, in love. To journey into the depths of our being is never easy, and for me it was at times painful; yet through it and because of it I have come to know myself and who I am, and who God is to me, at a far more profound level than previously – and I also know how much more there is still to be discovered!

Acknowledgements

This book is not a solo effort, but has grown out of the support and encouragement that I have received from many people.

The idea that the articles I had written for *Cathedral Life* could be the genesis for a book came through a conversation with Graham Rodger, editor of *Cathedral Life*; thank you for the encouragement you have given, and for the photograph on the back cover.

Thank you to Sam Dawson, manager of the former SPCK bookshop in Liverpool Cathedral for her unwavering enthusiasm, and for putting me in touch with Ruth McCurry. Thank you to Ruth and all at SPCK, for bringing into being something I never thought would be – a book in print!

Thank you to the Revd Peter Smith, and the members of his congregation at St Gabriel's, Aldersbrook, who tested out for me the Neighbourhood Prayer Walk, and for their comments. Also to those of Liverpool Cathedral who walked and prayed the Cathedral Prayer Walk, and ensured that I had east and west the right way round!

Thank you to the Revd Mark Williams, who invited me to speak at the training course for spiritual directors in St Albans Diocese, 'How to lead quiet days'; from this evolved Chapter 13.

Thank you to the Dean and Chapter of Liverpool Cathedral, for their support and permission to use the photograph from the Chapel of the Holy Spirit on the back cover.

Thank you to friends for their listening and words of wisdom along the way; to Mark, David, Peter, Rick, Ursula and Val. Also to my family – parents, sisters and brothers-in-law, nephews and nieces – for the enjoyment of their surprise when I told them about this book, and for sharing my joy with them when it came to be accepted and published.

Thank you to all those who have prayed and studied the Pathway to God course at St John, Ainsdale, Southport, and from the churches in the Walton Team, Liverpool.

Thank you to Bishop James for writing the Foreword and to Bishop David for his supportive comments.

Introduction

The path stretches out,
The journey begins to take shape,
Through hill and vale,
Through cloud, and
Illuminating light.
Where is it going?
Where does it lead?

The path winds on,
The journey, taken not alone,
Through pain and joy,
Through prayer, and
Amazing discovery:
Of self and of God
Of the voice that calls us – ever onwards.

'Let us pray . . .' – familiar words which we hear at probably every service and act of worship we attend, words which introduce the Collect and the Prayers of Intercession, and as we hear them we know that the prayer that follows is a prayer offered to God on behalf of the whole gathered community. With those words we prepare ourselves to pray; not alone but with others, and not necessarily for our own particular needs but for the needs of the wider world. Corporate prayer becomes the prayer of the gathered community of the Church, and for some this may be the only prayer offered to God that they pray, or have prayed for them. This gathered prayer is not only needed, but is vitally important as we look out from the confines of our own lives to the wider concerns of the rest of the world.

Yet as we travel the Pathway to God, how much time is given each day or each week in seeking to explore and discover, through prayer, the God who calls us to our own particular journey in faith – prayer that has God at the centre, and is prayed through the whole experience of our own lives? Prayer that may at first appear to be very self-indulgent, yet can open the doorway to a deeper faith and a more committed discipleship as we begin to see ourselves more clearly, and come to know more dearly the God who loves us.

From reading the Gospels we know that Jesus spent a lot of time in prayer, and not all of his prayer time was spent in the company of the others. Often, Jesus would escape the crowds to be alone in prayer with God his Father, and his time away in solitude and silence usually came after he had been very busy and very active. There is no record of how he prayed at this time, yet we can assume that through this prayer Jesus was renewed and refreshed for the ministry he was called to, and strengthened for the journey that lay ahead.

> Where do you go, Lord, to be quiet, be still?
> Where do you find peace away from others' needs,
> To feed and nourish the inner self,
> And so return, renewed and ready, and in good health
> Of body, and of soul; to listen and to give again?

To be alone in private prayer, for Jesus and for ourselves, is an important aspect of our Pathway to God and our journey through life, if we are to remain in tune with God, spiritually awake and ready to cope with all the demands of life. Through spending time alone with God in prayer we begin the journey inwards. This means that as we come to know ourselves better, with all of our strengths and weaknesses, and acknowledging all of our gifts and potential, we not only begin to see and love ourselves as we are seen and loved by God, but through this, our private prayer stretches out to embrace the whole of creation.

Introduction

The photograph of the kneeling Christ on the back cover shows Jesus at prayer. He is placed partway up the mountain in the midst of the natural world, and below can be seen the sea and the buildings of the village he has retreated from. It reminds us that time spent in personal prayer and in deepening our relationship with the God who calls us to prayer is not distanced from the rest of the world, but is very much a part of it. As our awareness of our own self and of God grows, so too does our awareness of the needs of the world, and our prayer naturally grows to encompass the cares of the world as much as those that are our own.

Jesus said, 'Ask, and it will be given to you; search, and you will find; knock, and the door will be opened for you' (Luke 11.9). The door is there, and like the door in the famous painting 'The Light of the World' by Holman Hunt, it is ready to be opened. In the painting, Jesus stands with a lighted lamp in one hand and the other hand is raised, knocking on the door; a door that has no handle on the outside. We are the ones with our hands on the door handle, we are the ones to open the door, and we are the ones to invite Jesus to enter.

Do we hear him knocking and do we invite him in? Once invited in, we will then be led along our own personal Pathway, at the speed we choose, and as we journey we can stop and pause whenever we like. For each of us the destination of the Pathway is God, and although we travel in the same direction, how we decide to pray, the types or styles of prayer we use as we follow the way in prayer, will be for each of us the same yet different, as we bring to the variety of our prayer the uniqueness of who we are.

Pause for prayer

The kneeling Christ

Kneeling, thoughtful, prayerful
knees on the hard earth
toes touching the ground
the ground of all being.

Peaceful, quiet,
only,
looking close at your face
can the furrows of deep compassion
be seen
etched in love
above the eyes
that see all, love all.

Kneeling Christ, stillness, quietness
vibrates forth from the
body, still
still active and being, reaching out
in silence
across the ages
encompassing.

Help me to kneel, thoughtful, prayerful
knees cushioned beneath
toes touching the ground,
the ground of my being.

1

Stepping out onto the Pathway

Our journey to, and with, God, takes us along a multifaceted Pathway. It is a Pathway littered with helpful directions, companions to share the walk with, and not forgetting the stopping-off places where we can rest awhile – all that is needed to enable us to live in faith and discipleship. The Pathway to God is a Pathway of relationship; a deepening of the relationship we have with God in Trinity, a journey into the embrace of the God who loves us. To venture out on this Pathway to God, the one important dimension upon which we need to focus is prayer. When prayer is at the heart of our relationship with God, we are attuned not only to God but to one another and to the whole of creation.

When we spend time in prayer we spend time with God. Although God is present with us, always and everywhere, it is in our prayer that we can become more aware of God's presence as we seek in a multitude of ways to communicate something of our inner longing, our heartfelt cries, our deep concerns, our hopes and dreams. Then, it is to have the faith and the courage to place all this into the hands of the Creator, who is the unfolder of all the potential within us that waits to be brought out from the depths of our inner self and into the true light of day. Paul writes to the Roman church in words of reassurance, then and now:

> Likewise the Spirit helps us in our weakness; for we do not know how to pray as we ought, but that very Spirit intercedes with sighs too deep for words. And God, who searches the heart, knows what is the mind of the Spirit . . . (Romans 8.26–27)

Even at those times when to pray is difficult, and the words we want seem far away or inadequate, God knows what it is that we want to say, and disentangles our often confused thoughts and mumbled words.

There will be times and places when we feel the closeness of God's touch, and others when God seems far away. As we journey along the Pathway to God, although we are not consciously praying at all times and in all places, there comes the growing realization that the whole of our life is a prayer; and we find that we do 'pray without ceasing' (1 Thessalonians 5.17)! This is because our prayer is our connection to and with God, it is our means of communication, our way of being in communion and relationship with God; and how this comes to be will be the same yet different for each one of us.

For some, it may be through written prayer, or those of our own making; it may be through the beauty of creation; through music or poetry; through the friendships and relationships we have; through the community of the church to which we belong; it may be being in the company of others or in the silence and solitude of our own seeking. Probably for each one of us, though, how we reach into God, and know God with us, will be as mixed and varied as each day is, just as we are from one another in our own uniqueness. So too our prayer, which through the faith we have, becomes increasingly and actively involved with the 'who we are' in our own uniqueness, as it is interwoven more and more into the fabric of our everyday lives.

Not surprisingly, there are many and varied ways of praying, and sometimes it can be a long and arduous journey to discover which way of praying is right for us at any given moment, and will bring us closer to the God we seek in our prayer. Depending upon what we are seeking, what our needs are, this will then affect the direction we take and the way of praying that is chosen; for example, to discover where God has been active over the past day or week or month, then the 'looking back to look forward' (Chapter 14) may help; to seek inner quietness, then to listen to a piece of music may enable this (Chapter 7); praying imaginatively through a Gospel passage (Chapter 4) can open up a conversation and so bring about a prayerful encounter with Jesus.

The Pathway to God holds along its route a prayer for every occasion, every life and world event – prayers written or those of our making, prayers inspired by music, the arts, creation, poetry, the Bible; prayers offered in silence or spoken aloud; prayers with tears of joy or tears of grief; prayers of petition or intercession, confession or thanksgiving; prayers for our own very personal journey into a deeper faith and relationships with God, prayers where we come to sit in the presence of God.

This mixed bag, which holds within it many different ways of praying, is there waiting to be discovered, and so too the prayers to be prayed. The 'how' we come to pray will depend upon our innermost needs and desires. Added to this are our own particular life experiences and changing situations that may mean that a different type or style of prayer is needed; and no way of prayer is 'wrong' if it enables us to continue the Pathway into God's presence and grow in faith.

As our journey through life leads us from one year to another, and as we grow and mature through all we experience, so too our prayer life should also grow and mature with us. We need to be stretched and challenged in all that we do, and the same applies to our lives in faith; we need to encounter God in different ways through prayer and praying, ways that will enable us to deepen our faith and our relationship with God; we need to come to know God more intimately and our selves more deeply as well. The prayers and the ways of praying we use when we first step out on this Pathway are not necessarily right for us in every stage of our lives, and it takes courage and faith to leave go of all that is familiar and to step out and try something new.

A place that is as good as any other to start with, is right at the very beginning! Although we can easily pray without any preparation at all, to simply pray with the words that come from within us, if we really desire to seek to spend time alone with God in Christ, quietly, silently, and to deepen our own personal relationship, then to spend some time in preparation may bring us closer to the God we seek.

Pause for prayer

God all encompassing

God all encompassing, God all loving:
    Open my eyes to see the way forward,
        to see you in all things, in all places.
    Open my eyes to hear your voice,
        to your Word spoken,
        to your call to me.
    Open my heart that I may come to dwell more deeply
in you
        as you dwell deep within me.
    Open my whole self to your love,
        with all its frailties and weaknesses,
        with all of its giftedness and potential.

Lord Jesus Christ,
    Take me, use me, change me,
    By the power of your Spirit, enflame my whole being,
    Expose my self to trust your call to follow you,
    Expose my fear that I may not be afraid,
    Expose my desire which yearns to love you more,
    Help me to know my self as I am known by you.

Guiding Spirit,
    Show me the Pathway to God,
    Bring to me quiet moments of prayer and reflection,
    Give to me the courage to look within,
        to have the peace to trust you
        in the times when prayer is hard,
    And the faith to be still and quiet in your presence.

2

Settling down to pray

Prayer can be described very simply as being our conversation with God, where there is both talking and listening. Yet prayer is so much more; in prayer we come to encounter the living God, and as we pray we enter into a new and hopefully deeper relationship with God in Trinity. Through our prayer, we can also discover more about our own self – our limitations, our giftedness, our Pathway through life. There are many ways in which we can pray, and prayer can be offered wherever we find ourselves.

There will be times when we pray as a gathered community, times when we will say a short, silent prayer as we journey through the day, and if we are to discover the way along our own very personal and individual Pathway to God, then we need to put some time aside to sit alone with God; this will then feed into all of our other meetings with God in prayer and in life. The more we come to know God in prayer, the more we come to know our selves, and the more we are enabled to reach out in faith and prayer to the rest of creation.

To give some of our time to God, and allow God the space and the time to be with us, is not a selfish indulgence but a vital part of deepening a relationship. One way in which we can deepen this relationship and awareness of God is through our time spent in one-to-one prayer with God.

First, and most importantly though, there needs to be the desire to reach out into the depths of God – do I want to be challenged, surprised, loved by God?

Second, and to use the well-known and much-used phrase it is to 'pray as you can and not as you can't.'

Third, prayer is a journey that doesn't have to be travelled all at one go; it is a journey of discovery – at times easy and joyful, and at other times difficult and dry.

So, how do we settle down to pray? Is there any need to prepare ourselves to pray?

Practical issues – a few questions to ask

- *Where do I pray?* One piece of advice I was given was to find a place at home that would be my 'prayer space'. This could be a chair, a particular room or part of a room that can be used as a place of retreat. It may take a few weeks or so to find the right place, but once this 'sacred space' has been discovered and used each time you seek to pray, it is surprising how it helps to quieten the mind to prayer.
- *How much time can I give*, realistically – each day or each week – to sit and pray? Will this be 10, 15, 20, 30 minutes, or more or less, not forgetting to add some extra minutes to review the time of prayer afterwards?
- *When is the best time* for me to be quiet and have the space needed to sit and pray? Is this in the morning, afternoon, evening or at night? Again, it may take a few weeks to find what is the right time, and this may change, depending upon other commitments.
- *What will help me to pray?* Do I want music, a candle, a cross, a picture to focus on, a Bible passage, paper, pens or paints? Gathering together anything that is to be used in the time of prayer will hopefully mean that the prayer time itself isn't interrupted by having to collect something that has been forgotten, especially if the prayer is a creative offering.
- *What will help me to become quiet before God?* What will I do if the phone rings?

- *What is the prayer to be prayed?* A part of the preparation needed as we come to settle ourselves to pray, is to ask the question: 'How am I going to pray? What is the prayer I desire at this moment?'

Don't feel that you can't change or make changes to the 'where', 'how', 'when' and 'what'; use them as a guideline and not as a definite rule. Particular home and personal circumstances, thoughts and feelings, outside issues and events can all have an effect on how we come to pray and why we come to pray. Our prayer will be more meaningful and prayerful, offered from the heart when we are able to do so, rather than forced out of us because it is the time decided on and set aside by us for prayer!

What else is needed?

- *Pen and paper.* This is helpful for two reasons. First, to jot down all the distracting thoughts that enter the mind as soon as you sit to pray! To write them down means they are not forgotten, and hopefully prevents them from continuing to be a distraction (more in Chapter 3). Second, at the end of the prayer time it can be helpful to spend about ten minutes reflecting on the prayer, and to note and make a journal of the Bible passages used, or piece of music, or poem, plus any particular thoughts and feelings that may be important, which you may want to bring back to prayer again; for example, did I feel close to God, joyful, tearful, happy; was I distracted, peaceful, unsettled?

  Making a note to *journal* the times of prayer can help us in our faith journey – as a reminder of how far we have travelled with God, to show any connecting threads in our story over the months and years; there may be an issue or a question, or a poem or Bible verse that recurs at regular intervals. There is no right or wrong way in which to journal the thoughts that come during prayer, nor does a note need to be made after every single prayer offered!

A journal is very personal, a treasure chest that will come to hold a myriad of thoughts and memories, reflections of life's important moments, snapshots of the journey with God. The journal is not a book of essays or carefully constructed sentences, but it is anything that expresses and keeps alive the feelings and thoughts that have been brought to the surface during a time of prayer. Words, phrases, pictures, doodles, colours – anything, as long as you know what it means yourself and will know again when you come to look at it at another time. However a journal is kept – notebook, scrapbook, odd bits of paper – it is an expression of the relationship between the one who keeps it and God, and therefore the Pathway of faith that is being walked.

- There also needs to be *a desire within* that will invite and allow God to guide us on the journey of faith, the Pathway to God – even if at times we feel very reluctant or uncertain.

Setting off

- *Decide on how you are going to pray.* For example, silence; contemplation: prayer in quietness with the minimal use of words or images; meditation: prayer using images or words as a way to focus upon God; through a Bible passage and imaginative contemplation: using the imagination to quietly enter into a biblical passage or scene and so to encounter God, to watch or participate, by allowing the Spirit to guide the thoughts, images, feelings, and any conversation (see Chapter 4).
- Then, *come to the place* that has been 'set aside' for prayer.
- *Become quiet and still within*, empty the mind of the busyness of the day, and allow God the freedom to fill that space; how

we do this will be different for each of us (see next chapter). Ask God to be with you in this time of prayer.

- *Read the Bible passage* or poem that you are using. There may be a word or a phrase that seems important to you; if so, repeat it, meditate upon it, and allow it to settle deep within you. Stay with that word or phrase for however long it feels right to do so, before moving on to another part of the Bible passage or poem, or by bringing the prayer time to a close. What does God say to you in the passage you have read, and in any particular word or phrase you may have focused upon? What do you say to God?

- *Draw the prayer time to a close* by using a prayer, maybe the Lord's Prayer, and give thanks to God for that time of prayer. Afterwards take some time to review the prayer time and write down anything you want to remember, as mentioned above; and the time used to journal and to reflect can be somewhere other than the 'prayer space'.

Pause for prayer

Be still and feel

Be still,
Be still
And feel.
    Feel the whisper of
    Breath that floats
    Through the air;
Calling, seeking,
Entwining, embracing
Creation,
All
As one.
    Feel God,
God's love,
God's touch,
God's Spirit,
    Cushioning, comforting,
    And be still.
Be still
And feel.
    Feel peace,
    God's peace.

3

As we come to pray: becoming still and quiet within

⟫━●━⟪

When a space has been created or found, a particular place where we can go to sit and be with God in prayer, then as we enter that space we do so knowing that we have come for nothing else but to pray and know God's presence surrounding us. Over time, if that place is used regularly, then simply by just going to sit there we begin to become aware of a growing inner stillness. Yet, before we come to any time of prayer, there needs to be the desire to become still and be quiet within; and then, in that stillness and quietness, to seek an encounter with God.

So we come and sit, having prepared ourselves and having decided what it is that we want to pray about; or maybe it is just to sit and see what happens. What usually happens next is the opposite to what we are seeking – instead of a quiet, still mind there is an overflow of words and thoughts, each competing with the other to keep our attention! We may never quite know where they all come from, as before sitting down to pray, these thoughts and words had no substance, no shape; they were just floating around unheard within the depths of our being, until that particular moment when we seek to be still with God: 'Have I got the meat out of the freezer?'; 'Don't forget to post that letter'; 'When did I say I'd phone . . . ?'; 'What time is it, and what time do I need to be out by?' The list is endless!

Out of the multitude of thoughts that comes to invade the mind, bringing with it a growing sense of restlessness instead of a deepening sense of peacefulness, there is the need to determine what is important and to be remembered, and what isn't. Having a pen and paper to hand is useful, so a note can be made of anything that isn't to be forgotten. Although the aim is to clear and empty our minds, to enable us to reach deep within and listen to and for the voice of God, the voice of God may be speaking to us in the distractions. There may be something that really has to be done there and then before we can find the peace and stillness in which to pray.

While at theological college, I began the preparation weeks of the Ignatian Spiritual Exercises, which meant giving a certain time each day to prayer and meeting regularly with my spiritual director as I discerned the movement and presence of God in my life. I can remember that on more than one occasion as I sat and closed my eyes to focus on praying, all I wanted to do was to close my eyes and go to sleep – which I did – and it took a while for me to accept that at that time sleep was needed more than the time of prayer was, and that sleep was also prayer!

Tiredness, as with any other distraction that takes us away from reaching the inner quietness and prayerfulness that we seek, does not mean that we have failed, nor need to feel guilty, because we have somehow not used the time put aside for God in the way we intended to. If the desire to encounter God in prayer was there, deep within, then prayer has still been offered – not in silence or quiet conversation perhaps, but rather with a heartfelt call of 'Help!' In our times of prayer, and in our times when we find it hard to pray, as in every moment of our lives, God takes us, and is with us, accepting us just as we are.

A few suggestions that may help in becoming still and quiet within

- *Become aware of the sounds* that fill or enter the room where you are: clocks ticking, cars passing by, your own breathing. Acknowledge all the various sounds and then let them be; let them come in to the stillness and be a part of it, hear them but try not to concentrate on them, so that the sounds do not then disturb the stillness.

- Breathing exercise: *become aware of the pattern of your breathing*, without changing it; and with each breath in, imagine breathing in the peace of God, and then breathe out any tension and distraction that lies within. It is very easy, as we seek to be still, to become increasingly aware of how we breathe, and more conscious of each breath taken, which can often result in breathing more quickly as we give more attention to our breathing, and so it is important to keep breathing evenly and normally, and not to let the breathing quicken unnaturally.

  So as you now breathe in and out allow the body to become as relaxed as you feel comfortable with. It may be helpful to move through each part of the body, beginning at the top of the head and then ending with the toes, relaxing each part of the body in turn, being aware of those places where there is any tension, and allowing the peace of God to travel through each and every fibre of the body; again only do this as far as you feel comfortable with. Or it may help to imagine that with every breath out, you breathe out any worry or concern, and with every breath you breathe in, you breathe in the love and peace of God.

- *Focus upon the flame of a lit candle*, the candle flame representing symbolically the light of Christ, and the light of illumination sought in our prayer; and if the mind begins to wander, look again at the flame to refocus yourself and your thoughts upon the prayer you are praying.

- *Using a picture or an icon* may be helpful in providing a visual focus that will enable the mind and the body to become still. It may also be used for the prayer itself, as the images, thoughts and feelings that the picture or the icon awakens within then lead us towards a prayer of contemplation or meditation, and so into an awareness of God's presence, and of our own journey of faith.

- *Music*: it can sometimes help to have a piece of quiet music playing in the background, and, as with the candle, if the mind wanders then focus upon the music again until the distractions fade away. If you are unused to total silence (and this probably includes many people), then to have music playing quietly in the background can be very helpful in enabling us to become quiet in God's presence; but choose the music carefully and pick a piece to play that you feel will echo the prayer you seek. For example, if you want to sit in silence with God, a quiet instrumental piece will probably be more conducive to creating an air of stillness than one full of discordant notes or lyrics. (More on music and silence will be found in Chapter 7.)

- *If you have a favourite word or phrase* from the Bible, a hymn or a poem that speaks to you of your relationship with God, then repeating this slowly over and over can also help to quieten the mind for prayer. In Chapter 12 we look at how to find the word or phrase – a motto – that is special to you.

There is of course the well-known adage: if at first you don't succeed, try, try and try again! Prayer, in all of its multifaceted forms, is or should be as natural to us as breathing, yet it is not always easy, and there will be times when we may not always know how to pray, when we feel unable to pray, and when our prayer is dry and arid. Perhaps what can sometimes be most difficult is this becoming quiet and finding the stillness within to enable us to reach out into God, and allow God to speak into the depths of our being. Yet, the more we try, the more we do our best in seeking God in a time of prayer, then a way will be found that is the right way for us; and God will do the rest!

Pause for prayer

Be still and listen

Be still,
    Listen to the sounds,
And hear
The hum of the heating system
The clock ticking in the background
    The bird singing
    The car passing by
The random thoughts
    Travelling through the mind;
And let them be.

Be still and listen
    And know the God who waits,
    And be at one,
        Complete
        In each other.
Sense in every fibre the touch
    Of the Spirit;
The voice of God's echo within,
    Words . . .
        And no words.
Hear and feel the song of the Spirit,
    God conversing,
    Speaking, communicating.

Be still and listen,
    Hear and feel
        And know God,
        Know self.

Be still and quiet:
'Speak Lord, for your servant listens.'

4

Using the imagination prayerfully

———⟫•◦•⟪———

In the previous chapter we looked at a few ways that may help us to find an inner stillness to enable us to become prayerful, not forgetting all the distractions that float, very quickly, to the surface to try and take our thoughts far away from the prayer we come to pray.

The prayer, or the way of praying that we seek at any given moment, may seem to be clearly obvious; at other times it may feel like putting your hand into a bag of folded-up pieces of paper and picking one at random and seeing what it says: 'Today your prayer is . . .'! But, depending upon what is happening within our own life and faith, and all that we are experiencing, all of this will have an effect upon the direction of the prayer we offer and the way of praying that we feel is right for that particular time and moment.

Moving to sit in the place which has been decided on for the time of prayer, knowing within the desire to meet with God, becoming still and quiet, we now come to unwrap some of the many ways of prayer that we can use on our Pathway to God.

One way of praying that encompasses both our own personal lives and our lives of faith, is through the use of our imagination. Children have a wonderful use of the imagination which they bring into story-telling and creative play, into every aspect of their life; and yet, as we grow in adulthood it often feels that somewhere along the way, and through the busy lives that we lead, it gets left behind – the unused gift. Yet within us lies an imagination that can be a means of encountering God in prayer.

Children look at the world around them with eyes that see its wonder and its possibilities – shapes in the clouds, a landscape that can be whatever they want it to be; all is transformed. This is the sight we need to regain, the sight of the inner imagination to look out and view the wonder of creation around us, and then to look within and bring to life the use of our imagination in the prayers we offer and pray.

To use the imagination in prayer – imaginative contemplation – was a way encouraged by the founder of the Jesuits, Ignatius of Loyola, to enter imaginatively into a story from the Gospels, to be there as a part of that story, and to see what can be discovered through it for our own journey in life and faith. It can be seen as a very personal way of prayer, as it is specifically a prayer of our own journey and our own very personal encounter with Jesus in prayer, yet as we discover more about our own self, who we are and who God is to us, then the more open we become to all that is happening in the wider world; the more in touch we are with our own inner being – our thinking and feeling – the better enabled we are to pray effectively from the heart for the concerns we have for the wider world. One way of praying feeds into another.

To pray imaginatively, is not only to use the mind, but to be creative as well, by calling upon all of the senses – sight, smell, touch, hearing and taste. As the words on the written page are entered into, we 'see' the event from within it, from a new dimension and perspective that in and through prayer we can make our own. As with any other way of praying, enter into this prayer only as far as you are comfortable in doing so; and again, it may take time and practice if it is to be a prayer of encounter and discovery.

I have heard many people say that they have no 'imagination' but will say that they often daydream, and one way I would describe imaginative contemplation is that it is prayerful daydreaming!

Others say that they cannot picture a scene inside themselves, yet have been surprised at all they have felt and discovered when they have prayed imaginatively – not 'seeing' a picture that looks like a photograph, but through the blurred shapes that come to form the picture within their imagination; and they themselves knew what each shape and blur represented within the story they were using for that time of prayer.

To begin with, choose a passage or story from the Gospels. As this isn't an academic exercise but prayer, the passage or story can be taken out of context; the verses before and after may help to set the overall scene, but in this case are not really important! This opens and frees the story, so we can bring to it the whole of ourselves (including the questions we have, the issues concerning us) and allow God to speak to us through the creativeness of our imagination. It is to allow our imagination in the prayer to guide us on this Pathway to God; and where we journey in our imagination through this prayer is determined by each person, and by God.

There is no wrong way of praying this prayer, because this is a prayer that reflects your own self, your own journey, your own life of faith, and it reflects where you are with God at this particular moment on your own personal journey, and in your relationship with God.

Having spent time to become still and quiet, read through the chosen passage or story slowly and attentively a few times to become familiar with it. Then put it to one side, close your eyes, and go through the story again in your mind, in your imagination, in your own way. Begin to picture the unfolding scene that surrounds the story:

- The *people* – their body language, clothes, actions; are they alone or with others in groups, are people walking down a road, or sitting on the ground, is it noisy or quiet?
- What is the *weather* like – hot, cold, warm, breezy?
- Are there any '*tastes in the air*' from the houses, from the lake, from the trees; what can you smell in the air?
- What is the surrounding *landscape* like – sandy, stony, countryside, village?
- As you build up this picture, place *yourself* within the scene and the story – where are you, what are you feeling, are you watching or taking part, what are the people in the story doing and who are they, how close are you to Jesus, do you speak to each other, what does he say to you and what do you say to Jesus? Let the story unfold before your eyes, and remain with the prayer for as long as you like and are comfortable with.
- Finish by *giving thanks* to God for that time of prayer.

Put some time aside after the end of this time of prayer, and make a note of the passage or story used and your own reflections, including within these notes any thoughts or questions it has raised, or answered. Also record your feelings and emotions – how comfortable you felt talking with Jesus, what you would have liked to say, what was the part you played, where you were in the scene, how close or far away from Jesus you were; anything you feel is important and want to remember or take back into prayer at another time.

Pause for prayer

Joining the Pathway and being present, prayerfully

Read through Matthew 14.22–33 – this follows the feeding of the
5,000. Become still and quiet in whatever way is helpful, offer the
time of prayer to God, and then, bringing together all of the
senses, thoughts, feelings conversations, imagine:

You are walking away from the crowds . . . away from Jesus,
who turns and heads for the mountain . . . the boat is there
ready and waiting . . . as you step into the boat . . . look back
at the place you have just come from, the people you have
been with . . . How do you feel as you get into the boat? . . .
Can you sit and rest or is there work to be done? . . . What
do you do and what do you see? . . . What do you notice
about the other disciples in the boat? . . . How do they look,
what are they saying, how are they feeling? . . . As the boat
goes further out to sea, sense the rising wind, feel, smell, the
spray of the waves . . . How comfortable do you feel at this
moment in the boat? . . . What are the thoughts passing
through your mind? . . . Do the disciples look concerned or
not? . . . Look up to the sky and see the early light of dawn,
and feel the wind that blows . . . become aware of the disciples gathering at one side of the boat . . . What do they see,
and how does this affect them, and you? . . . Jesus is there on
the water . . . hear his voice say 'Do not be afraid' . . . How do
the disciples respond? . . . Then hear Jesus say to Peter,
'Come' . . . Watch the look on the face of Peter, the others,
and on the face of Jesus . . . Hear the voice of Jesus say to
you, calling you by name, to 'come' . . . Do you step out? . . .
And when you do, how does this feel? . . . Reach out to take
the hand of Jesus . . . What does Jesus say to you? . . . What
do you say to Jesus? . . . Then be brought back into the boat
. . . How do you feel? . . . Do you carry on your conversation

with Jesus? . . . What do the other disciples do or say? . . . Then sense the wind fade away . . . as you arrive back on land and leave the disciples and Jesus to continue their journey, what will you take with you from this meeting as you continue your journey?

At the end of this time of prayer set aside a short period of time for reflection and note down anything that seemed important and to be remembered.

A few suggestions of Bible passages to use in prayer

Psalm 139 – The God who knows us

This is the God who knows who we are from the time before we were born, and from whom nothing can be hidden. The Psalmist writes of the God who is present everywhere, in the heights and in the depths, in our joys and in our sorrows. What does it feel like to be known and loved by God in this way?

Jeremiah 29.11–14 – The plans of God for our well-being

Within us all there is a deep potential of giftedness waiting to be born, to be used in our day-to-day life, and in the service of God. What are the plans and dreams that you have? What do you believe are the plans and dreams God has for you? In prayer can you seek out the direction in life that God is calling you to?

Matthew 14.22–33 – Jesus calls to us, 'Come'

The disciples are in the boat, afraid because of the storm, and then Jesus appears and calls out to Peter, 'Come', and Peter jumps out to go to him, until he realizes that he is walking on the water. If Jesus called out to you, how would you respond? In prayer, can you bring to Jesus any fears or doubts that you have? Often we can learn much through the doubts and questions we ask; Peter doubted, as would Thomas later, yet they were loved and enabled to serve in faith. In what way does Jesus call you to serve?

Mark 10.46–52 – Sight is given to Bartimaeus

Bartimaeus had the courage to call out to Jesus for healing, so that he could see again. However good your outer visual sight may be, how good is your inner sight – the looking within into the depths of who you are, seeking out the Spirit and the presence of God within? Jesus came to Bartimaeus with a question, 'What do you want me to do for you?' In prayer, imagine Jesus standing before you and asking you that same question; how do you respond and what do you say?

Luke 10.38–42 – Mary and Martha

At times we are very busy and at times we can sit and rest; there is work that has to be done, but we also need periods of quietness, in which to sit at the feet of Jesus. In prayer, consider who are you more like – Mary or Martha? Who would you like to be – Mary or Martha? What would it be like to hear Jesus say, come and sit, and let us talk together, as he did with Martha? What would it feel like to offer some service to Jesus, as Mary did in preparing a meal?

John 20.19–29 – Jesus stands before the disciples

The disciples hid themselves away in fear, keeping behind locked doors. What are the things, the issues that you hide away from, and lock away within the depths of yourself? Can you bring them in your prayer to Jesus who knows you better than yourself, who knows all of your fears and doubts and times of unbelief? In his love, Jesus comes to us and opens wide his arms in welcome.

John 21.1–24 – Breakfast on the beach

Jesus asks, 'Do you love me?' What is your answer to this question? 'Follow me' is the invitation of Jesus to you. How do you follow Jesus? In what way? How can you follow him more closely? 'Take care of my lambs. Feed my sheep.' How are you following that command of Jesus? What is it like to take time out and sit in friendship on the beach and share in the breakfast prepared for you by Jesus?

Matthew 28.16–20 – The great commission

Where is the Pathway that you are on, taking and leading you to? How do you feel about it? What is your part in continuing the work of Jesus? Where is God calling you to, and what to do? The passage concludes with the words that tell us that Jesus is with us, always, to the end of the age. What does this mean to you, and how does it make you feel?

A few other suggestions

Exodus 3.1–12	Moses meeting with God at the burning bush.
Psalm 51	Our need of forgiveness.
Psalm 121	The assurance of God's presence.
Isaiah 43.1–4	The deep love of God for us.
Jeremiah 1.4–10	Sent out to speak the word of the Lord.
Matthew 17.1–13	The Transfiguration, the glory of God revealed.
Mark 4.35–41	In the storms of life comes the peace of Jesus.
Mark 5.25–34	Healing, what needs to be healed in our life.
Luke 1.26–38	The annunciation, saying our 'Yes' to God.
Luke 24.13–35	The road to Emmaus, how we recognize Jesus with us.
John 4.1–15	The woman at the well; whoever comes to Jesus never thirsts.
John 13.1–17	Washing the feet in love, to serve and to be served.
John 20.11–18	The resurrection; Jesus appears to Mary, new life.
Philippians 4.4–9	Rejoicing in the peace of God.
Revelation 22.1–6	The river of life.

These are just a few ideas out of many, and there are passages within each book of the Bible that can be used in prayer and so bring us closer to God, and to a deeper understanding of the Pathway that we travel. Another example would be the nativity stories and those of the Passion which can be used in prayer at any time, but may become more meaningful when prayed 'in season'.

5

Prayer and imagination on the move: a prayer walk

—————➤●◄—————

When we looked at how we can use our imagination in prayer by placing ourselves within a Gospel story, the way we would do this would be to find a place to sit and be still. Now, though, we are on the move and our prayer is offered as we walk! We do not need to sit and be still every time when we pray; we can pray wherever we are and whatever we are doing – a walk along the beach, through the country or around the busy streets of a city can provide us with the space in which to enter a way of prayer which enfolds us, and unfolds from us; a prayer of thanksgiving for all of creation, and our own part within God's creation.

As we walk, we can pray our prayers of intercession, we can pray imaginatively, we can pray a prayer for our own personal journeying with God. As we walk, there can be a sense of greater freedom in which to pray, as all we see around us provides the inspiration for the prayer which is being offered.

To be outside in the open air and pray, to confront the vastness and variety of God's creation, plus all of the human-made structures and buildings, can be both challenging and exciting as we discover through the walk new aspects of how our life is tied up within, and connected to, the wider world. It is to look beyond what is visually seen and to seek out the presence and touch of God – in flower and tree, in brick and concrete. If you enjoy walking in the rain, then the colours and scents that come with the rain will probably open the Pathway to a different prayer than would be offered through the haze of a hot summer sun.

Where the walk takes place will affect to some degree the prayer prayed. Thoughts may journey in one direction along a walk in the country, while a walk around a city will bring other aspects to be prayed about to the surface. Before setting out on a prayer, the decision needs to be made about the direction or purpose of the time of prayer:

- Will it be a prayer of intercession brought about by the sights and people seen?
- Will it be a prayer of our own personal journey with God as we try to discern our own calling in life and faith – again allowing the sights around to have an impact on the way the prayer unfolds?
- Will it be a walk full of surprises, open totally to the thoughts and prayers as led by the Spirit to pray?

Whatever the focus of the prayer, and wherever the walk takes place, they each have elements in common.

- *Be aware of the weather*: feel the breeze or the warmth of the sun, the way the shadows move to change the colours of the landscape, look around for any movement of leaves on the trees, the ebb and flow of the tide if near the sea, clothes drying on a washing line.
- *Use your eyes*: the shapes and contours to be seen, the pattern of the clouds in the sky, the paving flags that make up the pavement, gardens attached to houses, the differing styles and sizes of buildings.
- *Touch and feel*: what does the ground beneath the feet feel like? If possible, touch and feel the brick of a building, the bark on a tree, the sand from the beach. How does all that is seen reflect something of your own thoughts and feelings?

If this walk is one of intercession, then as you walk, bring all that is seen to God in prayer – for example, the people who work in the area you walk in, the unknown people who live in the houses you walk past. Pray for the well-being of the place, for safety and security, hope and peace, for the schools, hospitals and local government.

If this is a prayer of your own life's journey, then use the landscape you see to inspire the prayer offered – draw into the prayer your family and friends, your work and leisure time, and any particular concerns that you have at that moment. What can be discovered of God as you walk?

The prayer walk could easily become a 'window walk' if you are unable to get outside. Sit near a window and take into your prayer all that you can see, and even that which can't be visually seen, but you know is there. The thoughts and suggestions for prayer offered in the 'Pause for Prayer' walks which follow next can be used as a guideline for a 'window walk' as you look outside; or even within the room where you are and the memories and the stories of your life that are held within that room.

Pause for prayer

A neighbourhood prayer walk

Each neighbourhood will offer different possibilities which will guide to some extent the prayer offered on the walk. The following is just one suggestion of a prayer walk, beginning at your own front door, and is a prayer for your own personal journey in faith – take and use what is relevant and meaningful to you, and adapt it to personalize your own faith journey, and the neighbourhood in which you live.

Allow yourself as much time as you need for the walk, so that you will not feel rushed. Also give yourself enough time to return home with space to reflect before entering again the 'normal routines of daily life'.

As you step out of the *front door* the walk begins. As you close the door, leaving the busy-ness of the day behind, ask God to accompany you on the walk, to open your eyes inwardly to the Spirit's presence and guidance, and outwardly to all that is to be seen within creation in this particular place.

Walk along the *pavement* and notice whether the paving stones are even or uneven, and if there are any cracks in the pavement, maybe with weeds growing in that small and confined space. The Christian Pathway is not guaranteed to be easy, and on the journey there are times when we need to delve deeply into our own thoughts and feelings, to bring them out into the open before God, and to acknowledge our own personal brokenness (cracks) and so seek the way to clean the path – which is our life – of its weeds. What are the areas in your life that are, maybe, causing you pain and anguish? What are your doubts and fears, and can you name your limitations and weaknesses? Consider what may need the healing touch of Jesus in your life and ask for the courage and the faith to bring all of this before him.

35

As you continue your walk, you will pass many *houses*. Who is your house a home to? Offer a prayer for the people who share your home; for members of your family; for friends. Whose home do you find a welcome in?

You may pass by *shops* on your way. Shops invite us in to buy; often this will be for the necessities of daily life, sometimes, shops will encourage us to treat ourselves. What is your most treasured possession? What is your most treasured memory? Take time to think about your hopes and dreams for your life – dream the possible and the impossible. What would your wildest dream be?

At some time on the walk a decision will have to be made about which direction you take. There may be a *pedestrian crossing*, or a set of *traffic lights*, or a road to cross. Is there anything in your life that requires an answer or a decision to be made? Is there something new you feel that God is calling you to undertake? Ask God to guide you in the right direction, and to help you to take that step to discover what the Pathway of faith may hold for you.

How much *traffic* has passed by you as you have walked? Some roads will be quiet, and others will have a continuous flow of traffic. Without realizing it we can often become overwhelmed by a steady flow of work and demands upon our time, and so neglect our need to rest and be quiet. How much time each week do you have to yourself? What are the commitments upon your time – for example, work, family, church, leisure, house, relaxation? Do you need to change anything in the way you live your life at the moment? How much time do you give to prayer, to reading your Bible, to exploring your faith journey and the Pathway that leads to a deeper relationship with the God who loves you?

As you walk, what can be seen of the wonders of creation? *Trees* change through the seasons of the year, shedding their leaves, and then slowly bringing into life new leaves. Is there anything that you need to let go of in your life to enable you to grow and mature as a person, or to allow you the time to take on a new commitment?

On *the way back home*, enjoy the walk and give thanks to God for this time of prayer. Once home, spend some time to reflect upon the walk and make a note (including the route you took) of anything that you may want to remember and perhaps bring to prayer at another time. To write down your thoughts and feelings means that they won't be forgotten.

Our church buildings also offer to us a space in which to sit and pray, but rather than sitting in just one place, the whole of the church is a Pathway to God, and as we walk around the building we will find that it can be a journey of both prayer and self-discovery: of God and of ourselves. The prayer walk on page 38 is based upon the Anglican cathedral in Liverpool, but can be adapted to fit any church. All churches have an entrance door, a font, an altar, an aisle. There may also be a library or book table, a Lady Chapel, choir stalls. Look at your own church building – how could you walk around and pray? The following prayer walk may provide suggestions for a prayer walk around your own church.

Pause for prayer

Cathedral prayer walk

A prayer walk will be different for each one of us. As our walk in life and in faith is one rooted in our own personal experiences, so too is our journey with God. It is a journey that is unique to us – our thoughts, feelings, words, silences, image of our self and of God, and our prayer, will reflect something of 'who we are'. As you walk around the Cathedral, take as much time as you need, stop and sit, look outwards to the building and inwards to the heart – where is God? There is no right or wrong way of praying on the walk – it is the prayer of the person walking and the God who walks alongside.

People who live in other cities can make up their own prayer walks through their own cathedrals.

The journey begins in *the well at the West Door*. Whenever we journey we carry with us far more baggage than we need to, and the journey of faith is no different. Take time to consider the baggage that places a burden upon your walk along the Pathway to God. What needs to be left at the door, maybe never to be collected again? Begin to walk through *the well*, pause for a moment at the top of the steps, and look down the length of the cathedral and the Pathway that stretches out in front.

Move to the *font* – the place of baptism, and our welcome into the church family; the beginning of our life in Christ. Can you remember your baptism? What does baptism, and to be baptized, mean to you today? Baptism is the beginning of our faith journey; how far have you travelled in faith?

From the font, look across to the *bookshop*. Bring to mind the people, the books read, that have helped, provided guidance, been influential on your own Pathway to God. Come to stand under the *nave bridge*, and look down the aisle.

Then begin to walk slowly down the *aisle*, taking in the space and size, the noisiness or quietness. What does it feel like to be here in this place?

As you walk down the aisle to the *chancel steps*, consider who walks with you in the journey you make; who do you turn to for support, guidance, in times of need – for example, family member, close friend, spiritual director? Who are the people who come to you for help? Who are the special people in your life?

Turn to the left to the *Chapel of the Holy Spirit*, and take time to sit for a while. We see Jesus kneeling in prayer, at one with God. Through our prayer we can discover more about ourselves and deepen our relationship with God. Who is the God you pray to? What is your image of God? How do you pray and what is your prayer life? What is the desire of your own personal prayer? Where do you go to seek tranquillity? What helps you become still in prayer and be more aware of the presence of God?

When you are ready, turn left out of the Chapel of the Holy Spirit, then up the steps at the end to pause outside the *Chapter House*. Looking through the gate, the painting on the wall is easily seen: Calvary, with Jesus on the cross. On our Pathway to God there will be times when we stray from the Pathway. What part does confession play in your faith journey? How easy is it to come before God and confess? How easy is it to accept God's love and forgiveness?

From the Chapter House, walk down the steps and pause in front of the *Education Centre*. To grow in faith and under-standing we need to read the Bible, use daily reading notes, join a study group or course. Is there something you would like to learn more about? Is there a way that you can fulfil this dream?

Continue up the steps and turn right and down the steps into the *Lady Chapel*. Another chance to sit and be still for a few moments. In the Lady Chapel is the statue of Mary, mother of Jesus. Does Mary have a part to play within your own prayer life? Mary's life was one of obedience and surprise, of joy and of sorrow. In our own lives there will be times of pain and hurt, joy and laughter. As you sit, remember a very special moment to give thanks to God for.

When you are ready, move out from the Lady Chapel. Come up the steps, which bring you to stand in front of the *High Altar*. Do you remember the day you were confirmed: what does confirmation mean to you? The reredos portrays Jesus with his disciples at the Last Supper, moving to Jesus in the garden of Gethsemane, and then on the cross at Calvary. Look at them and imagine being there with them in the Upper Room, to share with them the bread and wine; watching and waiting in the garden; to sit with the others at the foot of the cross – what does this feel like? What does it mean to you to be a disciple of Christ in the world of today, to partake of the Eucharist today? The disciples were called to serve and proclaim the Good News, and did so in many different ways. What are the gifts you have been blessed with? In what way has God asked and called you to use your giftedness?

From the *chancel*, maybe take time to sit, and look to the *choir*. Music can evoke many feelings. Is there a piece of music, or several, sacred or secular, that helps you to be in touch with yourself and with God? Standing in the choir, look down the full length of the Cathedral.

As you walk slowly down towards the nave, consider: what may God be calling you to do? What may God be asking of you at this moment? What do you ask of God? Walking through the nave and 'back into the world' and keeping in mind all your hopes and dreams, how do, or will, you live the gospel in the world?

After the prayer walk you may like to stop at the *Refectory* for refreshment and reflection. As you take a break, reflect over anything you may have discovered about yourself or

God. If you have come to some new understanding, what will you do with this new discovery, and how will it affect your Pathway to God?

6

Sacred space and sacred place

When you find a place in nature where your mind and heart find rest, then you have discovered a sanctuary for your soul.

(John O'Donohue, *Eternal Echoes*)

There are many places which offer to us the space in which to encounter the God who shares our own particular journey, of life and of faith. You may have been out to 'pray on the move' in your neighbourhood, or taken a walk around your church or cathedral, and through it discovered something new about yourself or about God; and the place which is that building, or neighbourhood area, may be, or have become, a special place, or to use the words of John O'Donohue, 'a sanctuary for your soul'.

Remembering that particular place of encounter in which God was felt lifts that place onto another level, making it special as it becomes a place of prayerful encounter, and so sacred, full of God's presence.

From this I would define 'place' as a general area or location, and 'space' as something more specific, as the space where we are, and where we encounter God; and it is through sensing the presence of God that the 'space' is transformed into a sacred space.

If a place is special because it holds in our memory an encounter with God, then as Philip Sheldrake writes in his book *Spaces for the Sacred*, that 'place is both *this, here and now*, and at the same time more than "this", a pointer to "elsewhere".' At the beginning of the book he writes, 'Place is space that has the capacity to be remembered and to evoke what is most precious.'

So there is a sense of locality and the present *here and now*, but also an awareness of the eternal, taking us to *elsewhere*, beyond all time into the presence of God, and to that which is *most precious*; which is discovering through our prayer the amazing depth of love God has for us, a love which enables us to love in return.

Once a place becomes sacred to us, it enters the narrative and story of who we are, and so becomes through our memory and imagination a way to inner stillness and prayer. As we sit to pray, the image of the place can be used as a stillness exercise, so as we visualize the place and its meaning within our memory that calls that place 'sacred space', then slowly it will bring to us an inner quietness as we remember the God encountered in that place.

A church or cathedral, as with any other place, offers the space to become sacred space, through the life that is lived out within it – the Christian life expressed in worship, music, prayer, welcome, friendship – and through our own very personal experiences and encounters with God. Bricks, stone and mortar provide a physical shape and space, but sensing the presence, power and love of God within it then transcends that physical space to sacred space.

Mountains within the Bible are seen as the place where God is met and encountered: Moses, Elijah, and in the New Testament, Jesus at his Transfiguration. To bring an image of the mountains to mind in prayer, for me, provides a sacred space of escape, a place of quietness – away from people and the phone! More than that, though, to be a truly sacred space that, through remembering and imagining it, enables prayer to be offered, it also needs to leave you afterwards with a sense of renewal and refreshment.

It is a sacred space that will help the journey of faith to develop, grow and deepen: the *here and now*, and a leading to the *else-where*.

A couple of years ago I went on a DIY retreat (comfort, good food and wine, and not forgetting prayer!) with friends to Northumbria, and we decided to follow some of the footsteps of St Cuthbert. Our day on Holy Island brought to us a sense of the sacred within the place of the island, especially in the agape we celebrated as we stood looking out over the sea and Inner Farne Islands; God was felt. We also went to see Cuthbert's Cave; cut out of the hillside, it stands amid trees with a view which looks down towards the sea. There was a stillness and a quietness that felt as though it could be physically touched; it was a place that to me, but maybe not to the others, spoke loudly of God's presence, and even the roar of a low-flying fighter jet didn't disturb the stillness of the place; the silence that had been broken apart just as quickly seemed to sweep back to embrace the air again.

A place that becomes a place of encounter and so a sacred space may not touch other people in the same way as ourselves, for we come to that place and space from within the context of our own lives and experiences, our own seeking of God. When we think about this sacred space within our Christian life and our own Pathway to God, we need also to remember and hold in balance the God who is revealed to us in the particular moments of our life and the God who is beyond our total knowing – God who is Emmanuel, incarnate, and God who is Other.

Is there a place that offers you a sacred space in which God is encountered, a place that enables an inner stillness to be found in which to come to prayer?

Sacred space is the place where we are, at any given and particular moment, but it is also the place we have reached on our own journey of faith; for we hold within us that sacredness which is the image of God. Whether a sacred place and space is a part of the world's physical reality, or the ideal held in our imaginations, it can only become something special if it opens the way to a personal and intimate encounter with God – the surroundings which enable us to be at ease and at peace with ourselves, which then provides us with a greater freedom to meet with God in prayer.

How often, though, is that awareness of a place of stillness and sacredness elusive, crowded out by the many things that have a call upon our time, all the things that have to be done – and done *now*? Maybe the place of sacred space and encounter is veiled from our sight for a reason. Maybe the Pathway only becomes clear if we step out with faith and the deep inner desire to come to that place of rest and renewal, to that place of prayer in which we give space to God, willing to be made vulnerable in God's presence.

Jesus says, 'Ask, and it will be given to you; search, and you will find; knock, and the door will be opened for you. For everyone who asks receives, and everyone who searches finds, and for everyone who knocks, the door will be opened' (Luke 11.9–10).

To enter into the sacred space of prayer, and to come to encounter both God and the self, there has to be the internal desire to find that place within our imagining, inside the memory and story of who we are. To enter totally we need to be prepared, as we do every time we come to God in prayer, to face the challenge of, and be open to, the presence of the God who calls us there to that place of sacred encounter. It also becomes a place of risk and vulnerability, as we offer more of ourselves and more of our lives into the hands of God; God who then sends us out to extend that space and place of encounter, in faith and in discipleship, sending us back out into the context of our own communities, and the world to which we belong.

Pause for prayer

Favourite things

In the song 'My Favourite Things' from *The Sound of Music*, 'raindrops on roses' is one of those 'favourite things'. To think about and ponder over in a time of prayer those 'favourite things' and naming what is very special to us can open a door to God, as we discover where and what brings to us a closer sense of the presence of God. This can also be a prayer of reflection and a prayer of remembering.

My favourite things – and why they are special:

Book:

Poem:

Bible passage or verse:

Music   – instrumental:

– 'with words':

– hymn or song:

Prayer:

Place:

Way to enable stillness:

Colour:

Anything else?

7

Music and silence

———•———

From the beginning you have created all things
and all your works echo the silent music of your praise.
(*Common Worship*, Eucharistic Prayer G)

We live in a very noisy world, and noise pervades even those places we call a sacred space, where we go in reality or within our imagination to encounter God! There seems to be no escape, and yet silence is something many seek: to find an oasis of silence within the busy-ness of our days. When silence is found, and with it a time to pray, there is still noise around us – the sound of our breathing, the clock ticking, cars passing by outside – but these we can call the silent sounds, sounds that need to be heard, yet not so they will then become a distraction from the time of prayer.

To spend time quietly, in silence, is important. It offers to us renewal and refreshment. To sit silently before God allows the peace of God to surround us, and opens the Pathway to our deeper listening to God. It was in the silence and not the noise that Elijah heard God speak. Later we will look at silence in the context of 'time out' – quiet days and retreats; now, though, we will look at silence united with music. This may appear to be something of a paradox, for music is always heard, and though it may be quietly offered and performed, it is never totally silent; yet when there is music, silence and quietness can often be found. For many, silence can only be found (or even endured) if there is music playing softly in the background, music that then enables and enriches the silence of our prayer.

The music we listen to prayerfully doesn't have to be what may be classed as 'sacred music', as any style of music can be used, although some care has to be taken. If a piece of music brings to mind a TV advert or programme, then it will be obvious that it may not be the best choice, when instead of God, the silent time of prayer is invaded with images of a particular brand of jeans or make of bread!

The music listened to in prayer need not be either classical or sacred, for the lyrics and tunes of some modern songs may also enable contemplation and prayer. By re-focusing what is meant to be general onto God it can then change the whole impact that the words of a song have – and no doubt move it a long way from the intention of the writer! I have used Elton John's song from *The Lion King*, 'Can You Feel the Love Tonight', at the end of a Good Friday evening meditation; without love there would have been no cross, and it is a transforming love that is offered and given by Jesus on that night to all, 'kings and vagabonds' alike.

Music is a very powerful medium, and can express our every emotion. Music can make us cry with sorrow or with joy, it can lift us into the heights of rejoicing, fill us with love, bring us to a depth of peacefulness that we may have thought impossible to know, and it can re-surface past memories – both happy and sad. We can sometimes 'feel' silence, but like music we cannot touch it physically; it has to be felt from within, from the heart and soul of our being; especially if, through music, we seek God.

As with the way we pray, which will be different for each of us, so the same applies to music, and a piece of music that takes one person through finite time to the eternal may not have quite the same effect on someone else. If you were to choose a piece of music that seems to bring the presence of God close to you, what would it be? Would it be an instrumental piece or one that has words as well? Reflecting on the words we hear as the music plays is yet another dimension of prayer open to us. Have you tried praying through the words of a hymn?

John O'Donohue in his book *Divine Beauty* writes:

> Music is the surest voice of silence. From the beginning silence and
> sound have been sisters. Music invites silence to its furthest inner
> depths and outer frontiers. The patience in which silence is eternally
> refined could only voice itself in music . . . Schubert once said that all
> music begins and ends in silence . . . unlike anything else in the world,
> music is neither image nor word and yet it can say and show more
> than a painting or a poem.

This is why we can use music in our times of silent prayer. The
silence is ours as we sit and allow the words and the music to
touch and reach our souls as we take from the music whatever is
needed at that particular time for ourselves – for our prayer, for
our journey with God, allowing the music to wrap itself around
us like a mantle. With each note we can quietly weave into the
overall rhythm, the images and words which express the prayer
we pray and offer.

One place where we find the weaving together of silence and
music is within the tradition of Choral Evensong, which we can
experience particularly in our cathedrals. The service of Evensong invites those present to worship in the silence, in the depths
of their own hearts, to pray their own prayers, in response to the
music and the liturgy that is being offered to God. We can
compare Evensong to the prayers of intercession. Within an act
of worship one person offers the prayers of intercession on
behalf of all. Likewise at Evensong, the music and the liturgy are
offered by the organist and choir, and in a smaller part by the
clergy, but on behalf of the whole of the gathered congregation.
The whole service is an invitation 'to be' rather than 'to do'.

Richard Shepherd, in *Flagships of the Spirit: Cathedrals in
Society*, puts it this way: 'In a cathedral service, every worshipper
need not be busy. In fact, one of the joys of cathedral worship is

that non-performers can be carried along without any exertion on their part.'

We don't need to know very much about the music being played, nor understand the words of an anthem or canticle that is sung in Latin; we are called to feel, to immerse ourselves in the music and to silently pray – with or without words. Then as we pray and allow the music to touch us with the presence of God, we are no longer passive but active, we participate but without any exertion!

Within the silence and the listening to music, whether at a service or alone at home, we may discover a Pathway to a deeper and more intimate prayer, and a Pathway that will enable us to listen, and hear, the voice of God speaking in time, and attuned to, the rhythm of our heartbeat. As well as speaking to God in our prayer we also need to listen, and in the silent company of music, we may slowly begin to hear the voice of God.

Pause for prayer

Music for prayer

From the music you have, select a piece to listen to within a time of prayer. If the music you have chosen has words, then it may help to have these written down, and to read them before coming to listen to the piece of music. It may also help to read them again afterwards.

Become quiet and still in whatever way is best for you, then listen to the music playing, and allow it to play through a couple of times. As you listen bring into the prayer time:

- Why that piece was chosen.
- If the music chosen has words, do the words reflect the prayer you want to pray?
- What mood or emotion the music itself reflects.
- How the music makes you feel, for example happy, sad, peaceful.
- How does this piece of music reflect something of God to you?
- How does it help you to pray (or not pray)?
- What thoughts come to the surface of your prayer through listening to the music.
- Does the music chosen help you to be still and quiet before God?
- Does the music help you to sense the presence of God with you?

8

Listening to God

Prayer, and praying, with music to listen to, can sometimes lead us to discover an inner silence which then provides a space for us in which to encounter God. As we engage with the music we hear and listen to, then in the quietness we may also hear the voice of God speak to us. Elijah had gone to the Mount of Horeb in the expectation of meeting with God, and of hearing God speak to him, but he doesn't say whether or not he was surprised that when he finally heard the voice of God speak to him, it came from within the stillness of silence, and not in the noise of the wind, earthquake or fire (1 Kings 19)!

The story of God calling out to Samuel in the night time is probably familiar. Samuel thinks it is Eli, and so he goes to find out what it is that Eli wants. Eventually Eli realizes that Samuel isn't hearing things but is hearing the voice of God; and the next time Samuel hears the call he is prepared, and so replies: 'Speak, for your servant is listening' (1 Samuel 3.10).

Prayer is often described as being a conversation, a conversation between ourselves and God. And just as often, this also means, or leads to the assumption, that we speak and it is God who is to listen! Think of a recent conversation you have had. Did one person speak and the other listen? Whenever we talk with someone there are elements, we hope, of both – one person speaks while the other listens. This way we learn, we share, we discover, we participate, and as we make our response so the conversation continues with each listening to the other, and giving space to the other; each speaking, listening, sharing, offloading, enabling.

Our time spent in prayer is our way of being in touch with

God, to enter more tangibly perhaps into God's presence, making that space both holy and sacred; special. Likewise, as with our conversations held with our friends, our prayerful communication and conversation with God also needs to be a two-way conversation – a conversation that is brought about by love, and by a deep need within us, to come into the presence of God; and also brought about through our growing awareness of God with us. In and through this listening to God, we can then become more aware of, and discern, the Spirit of God with us. This will help us when we are faced with frenetic, rushed and busy times, to reach within ourselves and feel the peace that is God.

What does it mean to listen as we pray, and how do we hear God speak?

You may have answered that question by saying, 'With great difficulty!' To hear God speak does not necessarily mean that we hear, as Samuel did, a voice speaking loudly in the night; or, as it is recorded in the Gospels, a voice calling out from heaven at the baptism of Jesus and at the Transfiguration – yet we may.

To 'hear' God is to be open to the presence of God; and to listen to and then 'hear' God may be something that we would prefer to avoid, just in case something is asked of us that we are not too sure about! If we don't listen, then we can go on with our lives without any challenge, without any change – but is this what our Christian faith and discipleship is really all about? To walk the Pathway to God is to walk a path of ongoing transformation, and this can only happen if we are open to the Spirit and listen to God 'speak' to us.

When we pray and when we listen in prayer we then awaken a multitude of possibilities that lie within us, maybe unknown or unacknowledged until that moment, as we come to travel on new Pathways or journey further along the Pathway already being walked. If we do not listen, then we risk missing out on something important. If we do not listen at all to God, only speak, then our lives will continue, maybe in peace and harmony; but will our true potential ever come to light, will we ever become the person God knows we are meant to be?

To listen is to be open and aware and responsive to the God who calls us, ready to be challenged, changed, confronted, comforted. To listen is to hear the voice of Jesus say to us, as he said to Bartimaeus, 'What do you want me to do for you?' To listen is to hear, and then we have to make a response.

Yet listening is more than 'hearing words'. If God does not always 'speak' to us in the form of words, how else can we 'hear' God?

- We can 'hear' God in the creation we see around us, and through all the elements of nature – from a small pebble shaped by the ebb and flow of the tide, to the awe-inspiring mountain ranges of looming presence and remote wildness.
- We can 'hear' God in the relationships we have with our friends and families, through our varied conversations, through our feelings and emotions.
- We can 'hear' God in the times when we ourselves are listened to, as we 'off-load' our concerns, share something of our lives, with another person; a person who listens to us in total acceptance and love.
- We can 'hear' God in those special moments when we feel totally at peace, and all is well with us and the world; in those moments when we sense the embrace of Spirit holding us in times of pain and distress and in times of love and joy; in those everyday events that make us smile; when we feel drawn to sit and pray; when we discover through the affirmation of others that a decision made has been the right one.

- We can 'hear' God as we read a familiar passage in the Bible as though for the first time, and within it see something new, receiving a new depth of understanding and clarity.
- We can 'hear' God through the books we read, through poetry, a film, or a piece of music, when it makes us stop in the realization of how that has had the power to reach deep within us, bringing us to a new awareness of God and our selves.

To listen to God is not always easy and it may take time to discern and come to know the way in which God speaks to us; and to listen may mean that we have to spend a little time discerning how we think, pray and feel. If God is made known to us at a deeper level than that of physical and vocal words, then we need to be able to delve within and open the way to 'reading' how we feel. To listen to God is to also listen to our own selves.

For example, how would you describe in your own experience of faith and life:

- What it is to be at peace, and what anxiety feels like.
- Joy, happiness, sadness, tiredness.
- When God seems very close, how do you know, how does this make you feel, and what is felt within when God appears to be far away?

All of this, then, needs to be brought into the context of our very mixed and varied ways of praying – our meeting with God, and our being met by God. As we do this we will slowly become aware of, and recognize, the touch of the Spirit's love and peace within and around us.

Pause for prayer

Listening

Become still in the way that is helpful for you. In the quietness imagine that you are sitting – anywhere you like – with Jesus at your side, then let a conversation begin to unfold; speak, but listen as well.

- What do you want to say to Jesus?
- What do you hear/feel in response?
- At the end of this time of prayer, offer a short prayer of thanksgiving and make a note of anything you want to remember.

Pause for reflection

How do we look, how far do we see?

When we seek on the Pathway to God, to deepen our relationship with God, then we need to be able, in our prayer and in our life, to listen and hear, in many different ways, God calling and speaking to us. As we listen to God we need also to listen to our selves. To come to understand our selves at depth, to see and know what makes us into the person we are, is not always an easy journey to make.

John O'Donohue writes in *Anam Cara*, 'The way you look at things is the most powerful force in shaping your life.' Our sense of self-worth and self-esteem, whether this is positive or negative, becomes the lens through which our inner vision is formulated, and how our outer vision takes in the view of the whole of creation that is set before us, and of our own creativity. It also affects how willing we are to come close enough to God in prayer, to listen and to hear God speak to us, in the context of our lives.

In prayerful listening to God:

- *What has been a 'powerful source in shaping your life' so far?*
- *What is the view you have of yourself?*

Our life is held within the whole movement of creation, and in a way becomes life only by our participation in the ongoing creativity of the nature of creation. This is a participation that is rarely static, for even when we, and creation itself, appear to rest in a time of passiveness, there remains still the ongoing flow of creative movement, keeping life alive.

What is the nature of creation and creativity within you? The seed of God's presence is sown within the fabric of our being, of 'who we are', and our giftedness and potential are interwoven through the whole of our lives. Yet how often does this giftedness of our creativity lie dormant, in the dark ground, without being lifted out into the light? To discover the nature of God within, of all we are and are meant to be, means that once it is known it is not to be dug back into the depths but nurtured, fed, loved, until it becomes a vibrant part of us, giving to us a life full of colour and variety.

In prayerful listening to God:

- *What gifts lie within waiting to be made use of?*
- *What gifts do you have that already add colour to your life, and the lives of others?*

Just as the colours of the created world give to it shape and form, so too the colours that make up our own lives provide substance, shape and illuminate something of the nature of who we are, and who God is to us. The colours we like or choose often reflect something of our personality and character. To discover the ever-changing colours that shade the palette of our inner nature is to become attuned to our feelings and emotions, to become more aware of God's presence with us personally, and in the context of the wider created world.

In prayerful listening to God:

- *What colours reflect who you are and who God is to you?*
- *What do the various colours mean or represent to you?*

9

As we listen and as we pray, who is the God we pray to?

<hr>

We are all unique, we all have our likes and dislikes, and our character and personality are shaped by the environment in which we live and have grown up – our family, our friendships, our work, our faith background and understanding. In many different ways all of this will have an effect upon how we 'see' God. This will also affect our feelings about how close to God we are comfortable in being; within the stillness of our prayer, whether we are silently listening or participating in conversation.

The image that we have of God can very easily be a reflection of some part of our own life – present or past – and it can be a difficult journey to change an understanding and perception of God, especially if it has been a more negative image than a positive one. As well as our image of God, our own self-image will also be reflected in the way we pray. So, to understand who God is to us may mean that we need to begin by trying to understand better who we are to our selves.

<hr>

- *How well do you know yourself – what makes you 'tick' and makes you into the person you are?*
- *What are your best qualities, what do you like best about yourself?*
- *What are your worse qualities, what do you like least about yourself?*

The more we can accept and love the person we are, acknowledging our many strengths and limitations, all that we are good at and not too good at, then the more the chances are that we will be able to approach God with love and a greater confidence and assurance; and be more open to accept and receive God's love as well.

This will be a love that enables us to grow in faith and in our uniqueness – a love that will help us to name and know, not as a failure, our weaknesses and limitation, but as a show of inner strength and acceptance of what we can and what we cannot do; to know, as well, that God can work in us with and through what we call our areas of weakness as much as through all that is our giftedness.

If you enjoy a good mystery play or story, then you know that as well as a complicated plot there are many red herrings along the way, and the odd skeleton or two hiding in the cupboard, not for public exposure, although we wait with eager anticipation for them to be brought out into the open! It seems to be a part of our human nature to keep a small bit of our selves to ourselves, and not for public viewing.

The more we get to know someone, the more of ourselves we unfold and allow them to see; yet to become close to another person is a risk and makes us vulnerable – to be rejected, laughed at – and so however close we are to another person, there will always be a part of our selves that we keep to ourselves.

When we trust someone in friendship, then we allow that person to see most, if not all, sides of our personality and character, which means we become open to the risk of vulnerability. Yet, it is with our closest friends that we can discover the full potential of possible and personal growth as we are encouraged and nurtured by their love and friendship. And we do the same for them. The same is true of our friendship and relationship with God.

To become open to God in a growing and committed relationship, to know the God who dwells within, is both risk and vulnerability, not only for us but for God also – as we can reject another's hand of friendship and love, so we can also reject and turn away from the love that God offers to us; a love that is offered to us in total freedom and acceptance.

For God to dwell in the whole of our being calls for a total giving of our self, a new way of living, an opening to God of all the hidden places within us, the boxes of clutter and dust that we have stored away in the depths of our inner selves. In prayer we can slowly begin a long-awaited spring clean, and in that prayer God will give to us the strength to cope with all that we find – the pain, hurts, sorrows, fears, as well as any new possibilities and new potential seeking to come out into the light; all that gives us the opportunity and the freedom to become all that we are called and meant to be.

- *When you pray, who is the God you pray to?*
- *What is your image of God?*
- *How comfortable are you to come before God, to listen and to hear the still, small voice, to feel the touch of the Spirit?*

Who is God to you?

The image that we have of God will probably change over the years as our own prayer life develops and our life of faith deepens; and not forgetting that the image we have may also be dependent upon any particular life experiences that are affecting us.

Which of the following sets of images of God reflects your own ideas of 'how you see God'? Who is the God who is revealed to you – in prayer, in faith?

- Distant, far away, remote, God who is not very interested in your life?

- Judging, watching, pointing an accusing finger at every failure and weakness, always giving jobs to be done, issuing orders and directions, and never totally pleased with the result?
- A rock, strength, support in times of need, but not to get too close to?
- A friend and comforter, powerful and mysterious, but offering a hand of acceptance and welcome?
- Intimate, close, loving, encouraging, wanting the very best for you, giving you the freedom to discover this total love at your own pace, one who calls you beloved?
- Gender, father, mother, both, neither, something Other than our hearts and minds can easily acknowledge or understand or put into words?

When God is revealed to us, then this can be in a number of ways – simply, through knowing who we are, our own self; through a growing realization and acceptance of God's love; through sharing our faith with others and being as Christ to them; through listening to those we trust and those who know us well and to God in our everyday lives; and through being carers and stewards of creation. Even more simply, it is through living a life of faith as best as we can, and loving one another as ourselves.

How we journey along the Pathway to God will depend upon the image we have of God, and the image we have of our own selves. When we pray, however hesitantly, we acknowledge our need of God, our belief in God who hears us; God who desires to dwell more deeply within us. This is not by seeking to control us or take over our lives by force, but gently, in love of us, accepting the little we can give, and waiting with an infinite patience until we are ready and able to give more of ourselves to such love that is God.

Pause for prayer

Images of God

- Begin by becoming still and quiet within, using whatever is the best way for you, then in the time of prayer, ponder on God by:
  - sitting quietly and waiting to hear whatever God may say to you;
  - writing down any words which express and describe God to you;
  - drawing or painting your image of God – noting the colours used, and what those colours mean to you in your relationship with God.
- Who is God to you?
- What is your image of God at this moment?
- Is this the image of God you really desire to have?
- What does it mean to you to pray and be with God?
- How much of the self can you place before God in prayer and in life?

Pause for reflection

'At home?'

What do the words 'At home' say to you? 'At home' reminds me of the period dramas on television, where at a certain time in the day, the lady of the house was 'at home' to visitors. Today we would probably telephone, text or email to arrange a date and a time to call, not arrive on the doorstep unannounced! Within the busy-ness of our days a visit may have to be planned and fitted into the diary, days, weeks and even months in advance; and we don't usually have the time to put aside a few hours each day to stay in at home waiting to see if anyone calls.

How 'at home' are we to God? Are we open to God at all hours, or just at a prearranged time and in a prearranged place? From reading the Gospels, we know that Jesus was constantly aware of God with him, and also of his need to escape from the crowds to rest in the silence of God, alone, and at times other than those set aside when everyone gathered for communal worship – 'while it was still very dark, he got up and went out to a deserted place, and there he prayed' (Mark 1.35).

In the relationship Jesus has with God, nothing is hidden and Jesus is open to God's call in and on his life. Here we have the ideal, which at the same time still holds within it a sense of reality as the human-ness of Jesus is brought to us often throughout the Gospels; yet we also know that Jesus is wholly 'at home' and at one with the God he meets with in prayer and in his life.

What about ourselves? Where and when and with whom are we truly ourselves? With different people we show a different facet of our identity, our being. I am one person to my nephews and nieces, another to my parents, another to the congregation, and another to my closest friends – the same but not quite, yet all are me. This will be true for all of us.

Yet we may also find that added onto this we begin to wear an invisible mask – a front to hide behind, to hide what we are feeling. Sometimes this is needed if we are to get through a difficult situation, but sometimes we wear it because we are not 'at home' with ourselves, with who we are. Yet, God is at home with us, regardless, unconditionally, always calling us into the embrace of love. To be 'at home' with ourselves and with God will take us along a Pathway of discovering our hopes and dreams, of bringing into being all that we are meant to be.

To be at home and open to the presence of God is to seek out the dream, the plans that God has planted within us, as we read in Jeremiah 29.11, 'For surely I know the plans I have for you, says the LORD, plans for your welfare and not for harm, to give you a future with hope.'

There is a dream, a plan, woven into the being of each one of us. As we become more 'at home' with the God who has planted this dream and plan, through love, within us, and as we become more 'at home' with ourselves, who we are, and know for ourselves that we are loved by God, then the plan, the dream will begin to unfold and take shape as we live our lives in time to the movement of the Spirit.

- *How at home are you with God?*
- *How at home are you with your self?*
- *What are your hopes and dreams?*

If we are to dream and come to know the plans that God has for us, and so be 'at home' with them, then we need to spend time with God; to talk with God, and to listen to the voice of God speaking to us. We need to move away from the crowds as Jesus did, and seek in the silence of our prayer the relationship of love offered to us, to reach out, and maybe to take the risk and to welcome this gift of love and friendship from God.

For some, to accept and know God's love may be easy, for others more difficult, and this will depend upon our perceptions and images that we have of God and of our self, all of which will be fed into the way we come before God in prayer. Yet, one facet of the dream that God has for us is that we come to know this love, however slowly and hesitantly we open up more of ourselves to the love offered and given. God waits, though, with an infinite patience and tenderness, until we are ready to totally know the gift of this love in the whole of our lives.

10

Potholes in the Pathway

———▶◦◀———

As we follow the way of God in prayer and faith, and bring our prayer and faith into every aspect of our day-to-day lives, it doesn't mean that we will always have a smooth and untroubled Pathway. As we journey, there will be many obstacles and problems to be dealt with, difficult decisions to be made, times when we feel very vulnerable and in need of help and guidance. There will also be times on the journey when we come to the realization that we haven't done the things we said we would do, or have spoken in haste without thinking what the effects of those words may be.

Somewhere along the Pathway we will eventually find ourselves falling into a pothole, not just once but many times on the journey we undertake! These will be potholes of our own making, and ones we fall into unintentionally, unaware perhaps that we have fallen, until we have a time of reflection. The potholes remind us of our need to include the prayers of confession in our overall journey along the Pathway of faith.

There will be many occasions when we stray from the path we follow, and this could be as simple as being neglectful and not doing something that we have promised to do; not being as sympathetic as we could be; allowing our anger to get the better of us. It is all of those times when, to some degree or another, an element of forgiveness is required – of ourselves, to and from the person we may have offended or hurt, and of God; when we need to seek out once more the inner peacefulness that only God can give, and to know and accept that we are forgiven.

'Sorry' is such a very small word, yet at times it can be the most difficult one to say! It can take courage to face another person, to say 'Sorry' and ask for their forgiveness. Yet, when we realize that we need to say 'Sorry' for something that we have or have not done, we then begin the journey of stepping out of the pothole. There is also a sense of renewal and freedom that comes from saying 'Sorry' – a new beginning.

- *How easy is it to confess to God and seek God's forgiveness?*
- *How easy is it to know that we are forgiven?*
- *Is to confess, or make your confession, a part of your own personal prayer life, or just a part of the corporate act of worship?*

Prayers of penitence and confession which ask us to be open about all that needs forgiving in our lives, are both communal and personal. They are communal as we gather together in church and with one voice we confess our sins in penitence and faith, firmly resolved to keep God's commandments and to live in love and peace with all. It becomes personal as we pray silently within this community, to ask God's forgiveness as we confess our own sins. It is also personal as we bring into our private times of prayer an acknowledgement of all that needs to be healed through the forgiving love of God.

Central to both, the communal and the private, is the saying sorry to God, and so to come before God in confession is another way of praying on the Pathway to God. To grow in the faith that is being nurtured within, and to deepen the relationship that we have with God, requires us to make a response to the love God has for us.

Confession, knowing that we need to say sorry, shows that we are aware of the potholes we fall into, and that we recognize that if we are to walk the Pathway, then it means that along the way a certain amount of pruning will take place – not once but often. There are a number of ways in which we can bring into our own personal prayer life, prayers of confession or 'offloading' to God.

Within daily or weekly prayer

To bring before God all that we have forgotten and neglected, all that needs to be healed in our lives, can be included within the pattern of our daily or weekly prayer. This does not necessarily need to be offered by using a formal written prayer, but through our own words spoken quietly and simply from the heart, asking God's forgiveness and help for the day that lies ahead. In the 'Pause for prayer' at the end of Chapter 14 we look at the prayer of 'Looking back to look forward' and this review of the day can become a prayerful way of bringing everything that has happened in the day to God – the good and the not so good.

In the Order for Night Prayer or Compline (*Common Worship – Daily Prayer*) there is included the following prayer:

Most merciful God,
we confess to you,
before the whole company of heaven and one another,
that we have sinned in thought, word, and deed
and in what we have failed to do.
Forgive us our sins,
heal us by your Spirit
and raise us to new life in Christ. Amen.

If the word 'we' is changed to 'I', 'our' to 'my', and 'us' to 'me', then this becomes a very personal prayer, and before asking for forgiveness, anything that needs us to say 'Sorry' for, can be included. This is a prayer that calls us to be open and honest, and to have the faith to leave all that we say with God; then it is to continue the journey in peace, and hopefully not carrying the burden of what has been confessed any more.

By talking to another person, and being listened to

This can be in a number of ways:

- Meeting with a priest, one to one, in the sacrament of confession and absolution. Formal confession is not a part of all church traditions, and those who do seek this will decide how often they go to meet and talk, and confess. Time will be given to explore what needs to be confessed, guidance may be offered, the prayers are heard, and then the forgiveness of God is given.
- Meeting one to one on a regular basis (four or more times in a year) with a spiritual director. This is a person who will listen as you explore the whole of your life and faith – your prayer life, where and how you feel God is guiding you, the stresses and strains of daily life, everything that affects your relationship with God and the wider world.
- Within a prayer group. Where there is both trust and confidence in a group, then there will be the freedom to 'offload' and speak from the heart, and to be heard in an atmosphere of prayer and acceptance.

Whenever we meet to talk about our life and faith with another person, then God is present as well, and whenever we speak of all that lies deep within us, then we are confessing and witnessing to all that we believe in and hold dear, all that is important to us. In this listening we may find that there are no answers given, no solutions to a problem offered; yet, as we speak and bring it out into the open through our words, it often happens that we discover for ourselves, and then come to, a clearer perspective and clarity of understanding and direction than we had previously.

This could be seen as the hidden value in speaking one to one, as we explore our feelings and thoughts in the listening presence of another, who accepts us in love. It calls for a relationship embraced within it a sense of safety in knowing that whatever is said, it will be heard; there needs to be trust in the person who listens to us, in ourself to be honest, and in God, that we are loved by God, unconditionally.

A poem that has been a part of my Pathway to God for many years is 'Love' by George Herbert. The poem takes us through the Eucharist, the Holy Communion, as Love, God, calls us to join the meal being offered. There is the acknowledgement of the sin that lies heavy in the soul, but Love does not give up, and speaks of the forgiveness that can take, and does take, our sins away. We are the ones to make our response to this Love of total acceptance.

Love bade me welcome: yet my soul drew back,
Guilty of dust and sin.
But quick-eyed Love, observing me grow slack
From my first entrance in,
Drew nearer to me, sweetly questioning,
If I lacked anything.

A guest, I answered, worthy to be here:
Love said, You shall be he.
I the unkind, ungrateful? Ah my dear,
I cannot look on thee.
Love took my hand, and smiling did reply,
Who made the eyes but I?

Truth Lord, but I have marred them: let my shame
Go where it doth deserve.
And know you not, says Love, who bore the blame?
My dear, then I will serve.
You must sit down, says Love, and taste my meat:
So I did sit and eat.

(George Herbert, *The Country Parson, The Temple*)

We are called to partake in life and all that God offers us, and if we truly say sorry from the depths of hearts, and do our very best to live in the way of God, then we will know God's forgiveness. The hardest part after speaking of all that lies within is to accept that we are forgiven, and to accept and know God's love of us.

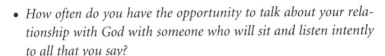

- *How often do you have the opportunity to talk about your relationship with God with someone who will sit and listen intently to all that you say?*
- *How easy is it to accept that God loves you?*

Pause for prayer

In John's Gospel we read:

> I am the true vine, and my Father is the vine-grower. He removes
> every branch in me that bears no fruit. Every branch that bears fruit
> he prunes to make it bear more fruit. You have already been cleansed
> by the word that I have spoken to you. Abide in me as I abide in you.
> Just as the branch cannot bear fruit by itself unless it abides in the
> vine, neither can you unless you abide in me. I am the vine, you are
> the branches. Those who abide in me and I in them bear much fruit,
> because apart from me you can do nothing. (15.1–5)

The branches are stronger through the pruning they receive,
which removes all that saps their strength and prevents full
growth. Renewed by the love of God through the forgiveness
given, then we go out energized and refreshed, and hopefully
strengthened in faith as we come to abide more deeply in God,
and God in us.

- *How has God 'pruned' your life to bring forth something new?*
- *What do these verses 'say' to you as you travel your own particular Pathway to God?*

Pause for prayer

Love called
(inspired by the George Herbert poem 'Love')

Love called out to me,
    to come
from without, beyond,
and join the Light
that sets afire
the deepest recesses of my inner self;
my heart and life.

And I,
    though unworthy be to come
so close to you, my God
can only move,
and forward journey on,
to seek, to search,
the Eternal and the only One;
my beginning and my end
within whom rests my heart's desire
to be in Light,
in Love itself,
held within Love's Trinity.

Love called out to me,
    to come
to God as Man
and join the Light in guiding others
to the Star of Bethlehem;
Emmanuel.

And I,
    though unsure at first to come
and follow such a way as this
can only move
and forward journey on
to be, to listen, to the world around,
and show Christ's Star and Cross
make known his life and death
for each and all;
to be a light in Light itself
helped by Love's Trinity.

11

Enjoying the view?

———⇒►-◦-◄⇐———

The thoughts and prayers offered within this book have at their heart the personal journey of the individual. We all follow the Pathway which leads to God, in our own particular way, and in a way that will help us to deepen the faith that we have as we discover more about ourselves and the God who has called us to this Pathway. Yet, as we look within ourselves we need also to take a wider view, to look out to the wider perspective of the world in which we live. We need to look around us as we journey; moving from the inner Pathway of personal prayer to the outer Pathway of intercessory prayer.

Most people, if asked to name some of the different ways of praying, would probably put the prayers of intercession first. Intercessory prayer is where we place our needs to one side, and so pray not for ourselves but for others and their needs. Prayers of intercession can be prayed by us at home, on our own, and will be offered and prayed by the gathered community in church services.

When we pray the prayers of intercession we show that we care about the people and the situations mentioned in our prayers, and that we hold them before God in love. Through our intercessory prayers we declare that we are not standing at a distance from the world, just looking and enjoying the view, but that we want to be active within the world, to make it a better place, so that everyone can enjoy the view – in peace and with justice and equality, love and hope.

Our prayers of intercession could be described as being a going out beyond the self to encompass the whole of creation, and to unite and present every aspect of life, before and to God, in love and faith. As we pray our prayers, whether alone or within a church service, we unite them with those being offered throughout the world; not one voice but many – voices lifted to God with the hope and the faith that God hears and will act upon the prayers we pray.

It may be that the least and the most that we can do is to pray, and to bring all that we see and hear from our TV screens, and life around us, into the presence of God with words that flow from the heart, the centre of our being. It is also very easy to find ourselves in 'compassionate overload' due to the many images and stories that come from around the world and into our own homes; yet even to feel and sense another's pain and need, however difficult it may be for us to bring this into words in our prayers, is still prayer. It is prayer because it touches our hearts. This is where our intercessionary prayer is grounded and evolves from the heart. If we did not feel something within us, or if we did not care, then we could not pray effectively.

Intercessionary prayers are found throughout the Bible. Abraham prays to God, or pleads, for the safety of the righteous in Sodom (Genesis 18.2–33); Moses intercedes on behalf of the people of Israel, and implores God not to bring disaster upon them (Exodus 32.11–14); Samuel was asked by the people to pray for them to God (1 Samuel 12.19).

Jesus teaches his disciples to pray the Lord's Prayer (Luke 11.1–4) and tells them to persevere: 'Ask, and it will be given to you; search, and you will find; knock, and the door will be opened for you' (Luke 11.9). In John's Gospel (chapter 17) we find the 'high priestly prayer', as Jesus prays for his disciples, that they may be equipped for all they will be called to do in his name. The whole of Jesus' life can be viewed as one of intercession as he looked not to himself but always to the needs of those around him. The passages from Paul's letter to the Ephesians, which can be found at the end of this book, are a part of his intercession that the people will continue to grow in faith and come to know more deeply the love of God.

When we offer our intercessionary prayers in church they usually include prayers for the church, local and national; for the whole of creation and those in authority; for the local community; for those in need, those who suffer; and for those who have gone before us, the communion of saints. The prayers may be led by one person, but they are offered on behalf of the whole community, and as we listen to the prayers we make them our own by responding, as together we say 'Amen' or 'Hear our prayer'. Included in the intercessions can be prayers to reflect the season of the year, and also a time of silence which can provide the space to silently pray our own prayers as well.

How do we pray our prayers of intercession at home? If different people lead the prayers in church then each will pray them in their own particular style; yet at home on our own it can very easily feel that, on most days perhaps, our prayers of intercession come to resemble our shopping list! Here are two suggestions. First, Paul in his letter to the Thessalonians writes and encourages them to 'pray without ceasing' (1 Thessalonians 5.17). For a moment, bring to mind someone you care for very much. At times we will think, consciously, about that person; but for most of the time we know and remember them, we carry them deep within us, without consciously thinking about them. In prayer we *pray without ceasing* all day and every day – hopefully. There will be times when, as a gathered community, we offer our communal prayers, including our intercessions, to God; and times when we pray on our own, quietly held in God's presence.

Our faith tells us that God is Emmanuel, with us always and everywhere; as we come to know this, in faith, then the whole of life becomes prayer without ceasing. Vocal and non-vocal prayer is offered as we do our best to live in the truth of the gospel, as all that we see around us is brought through our feelings and emotions into our intercessionary prayers. The prayers we offer may be a simply said 'arrow prayer' (see Chapter 12), or giving a friend we know in need a hug.

Second, it may help to write a list! How this list is put together will depend on your own prayer life. If you have a time of prayer each day or a couple of days each week, then decide if you want to include intercessionary prayers each time you come to pray. The time given to intercessionary prayer can be as short or as long as you feel is needed.

Using, for an example, five days when intercessionary prayer is included in your daily prayer time, on a piece of paper, divide it into five sections, and maybe put the day at the top. Then for each day decide what will be the focus of your intercessions; so that over the course of the five days all areas of intercession are covered. For example:

Monday:	Family.
Tuesday:	The needs of the world.
Wednesday:	The needs of the community.
Thursday:	Place of work, groups you belong to.
Friday:	Friends.

To focus on one particular area helps to lessen the sense of offering a shopping list. The list, though, is only a guideline, and there will be times when world or personal events need to be brought to God in prayer, not just on one day but on several. The seasons of the year may also be reflected, as Lent and Christmas bring to mind particular prayers to be prayed. A list is an aid to remembering, not a rule.

Pause for prayer

The Lord's Prayer is a prayer that we will all be familiar with, and it is a prayer that encompasses both the personal and the communal, our own selves and the wider world. We can pray through the words of the prayer as it is given, or we can take each line or each phrase in turn, and allow those words to become the foundation of a prayer of intercession.

Our Father, who art in heaven, hallowed be thy name;

We remember through these words that it is God we lift our prayers to, and that as we pray we become open to the presence of God in our lives and ask God to be with us as we pray.

Thy kingdom come; thy will be done; on earth as it is in heaven.

We pray for the world, that it may know the peace, love and healing of God's kingdom; we pray for a transformation in the world that will enable all to live in harmony.

Give us this day our daily bread.

We pray for all that is provided for our needs; for all that needs to be shared more equally with others; for an end to poverty, for a greater social and environmental awareness.

And forgive us our trespasses, as we forgive those who trespass against us.

We pray for all areas of life that need healing from the hurts and pains caused by the actions of others, and by ourselves.

And lead us not into temptation; but deliver us from evil.

We pray that we may be strengthened in faith, and enabled to witness to the truth of Christ in all situations and on every occasion.

For thine is the kingdom, the power and the glory, for ever and ever. Amen.

We remember again that we are a small part of God's creation, yet called to participate within that creation; and it is to God we pray, and in saying 'Amen' we acknowledge the prayers we offer and that all that has been prayed is what we want to be.

12

Life in the fast lane: when the Pathway becomes a motorway!

<hr>

One children's story tells of a race between the hare and the tortoise. The hare rushes off, eager to start and just as eager to keep on going to the end, and of course to win. The tortoise sets off at a slow pace, and surprisingly passes the hare and comes in first. If we rush through life at such a quick pace then we could soon find ourselves exhausted, 'burnt out', as the hare did.

The slow and sedate speed of the tortoise may not be possible all of the time, but there need to be times of rest within our days, weeks and months in which we can slow down enough to at least catch our breath and clear our mind; and also to have time to talk and be with family and friends. Ensuring that there is a space in which to step aside from the busy-ness of life – for prayer and for the self – will then provide the inner energy needed to keep on going when the pace quickens.

When we come to listen to God in our times of prayer it may be thought that to listen and to pray means that we have to be still and quiet, but what happens when the days seem to rush past so quickly that we feel we have no time to pray, let alone listen?

Feet pause on the Pathway
  Amidst the rush and the clutter,
    And the head fast-tracks to a large full stop
    Without stopping, another job done!
  The heart seeks the feet, resting,
  Torn between the two,
Again the head controls – and wins,
  And the feet take up the pace;
  Reluctantly, again.

The Pathway to God that we have been travelling is a journey of prayer focused upon our own very personal relationship with God, and to discover more about our self, who we are, and our faith and who God is to us. It is a Pathway that we can travel along at any speed we like, but what happens to us spiritually when time rushes by so quickly that we hardly realize where the days, weeks or months have gone?

When this happens, then we may feel that our prayer life seems to have come to a full stop or red light, or we find ourselves wandering around in a maze of work and family commitments: and we realize that we have lost sight of the way out! Life continues as we hurtle on, past all of the 'speed cameras' warning us to slow down; and in this busy-ness, our prayer, or at least those special times put aside for God, are probably the first to disappear in the rush.

It is far easier to 'get out' of the routine or practice of giving space and time to God in prayer than it is to begin it! If the pressures and stresses placed upon the whole of our lives increase, then there will come a time when we feel that enough is enough, and there is so little free time that we keep those precious minutes for ourselves and not for prayer. If we are not careful, though, it is very easy to lose sight of God, and the Pathway to God. Not only can our relationship with God grow distant, but also that which we have with our family and friends.

Motorways are very useful roads, and on most there are now signs which remind the driver of the importance of taking a rest every couple of hours, and service stations to stop at, in which to pause and take a rest on the journey. When the days are very busy, how can we ensure that we find at least a few moments to stop and pause, in prayer? If you have realized that the time you give to prayer on your Pathway to God has ground to a halt, then the first question to ask is, 'Why?'

Has prayer come to a halt because it no longer brings to you something of the peace and presence of God? Has prayer become meaningless, boring, a burden? If this seems to be the reason, then it may be the time to try a different approach to prayer, a different way of praying. Taking time off to go away on holiday gives us a break from the routine of life, and hopefully we come back renewed and energized. Sometimes just by changing the pattern and the way of praying can be like taking a holiday, and in doing so we may discover some new aspect of ourselves and of God.

Has prayer stopped because you are busy and preoccupied – and is this short term or long term? It is important, though, not to feel guilty about not being able to spend as much time (or any) in prayer as we would like when circumstances beyond our immediate control appear to suddenly come and take over our lives. It is also important to note whether or not there is any particular worry or concern that is affecting your life, for this too can make coming to pray difficult.

Whatever the reason, if it has been noted that the prayer once looked forward to and enjoyed is no longer taking place or enjoyable, then it may help to talk it through with a person you trust: a close friend, clergy, or a spiritual director. To bring our thoughts out into the open can often help to place into perspective all that is taking place in life, and provide some clarity of understanding and a way forward. To be listened to in this way could be called another way of prayer, as we seek a better view of God in our lives.

Having asked the initial question 'Why?', the next, regardless of how busy you are, will be: 'Is there still the desire to pray and spend time with God?' If the desire to pray remains, then prayer is still offered by us, even if we don't realize it, even if we do not give the time we would like to or feel we need to give. Our prayer and our life are interwoven, and the desire to pray which comes from the heart may then find itself being expressed simply through our remembering God with us (however fleeting!). It is the realization that God is present with us, always, and can be experienced and felt in our activity and busy-ness, as well as in the stillness and quietness. There will also be times when we need the courage to rest upon the prayers of others; it is not always easy to pray during illness, in very stressful situations, when we feel heavily laden with responsibility at work and for the family.

A few prayer suggestions for those days when the Pathway has become a motorway

- *Arrow prayers.* These are quick and very short prayers. It may be to say 'Thank you' for the parking space and traffic lights on green! It can also be a prayer asking for help, as Peter said once he had stepped out on the water to walk to Jesus, 'Lord, help me!' Arrow prayers are prayers we can fit into the busiest of days, into those few minutes as we stand waiting for the kettle to boil. Although it may not feel as though this is a prayer, it is still a calling upon God, hopefully coming from deep within where there is the desire to pray and the acknowledgement that God hears us, always; and, however short our prayers are, accepts all that is offered.

- *Reorganizing or reusing the minutes in the day.* Is there any time within the day which could be reused to provide an oasis to rest by? One person I know had about 15 minutes in the car each day waiting for her children to come out of school, and she decided this was the time that could be used for prayer. Deciding that the office of Evening Prayer wasn't what she really wanted, she put together a few prayers on a bookmark, placed this in her Bible and used both in prayer in the car. Someone else escaped to the bathroom to soak in the bath to pray, the only place where she could find peace away from the family!

- *Sunday services.* For many, the beginning of a Sunday service is the time to chat and catch up on all the news that has happened over the past week. If the rest of the week is so busy that your own prayer ends up at the bottom of the list of things to do, then it may help to try and come about ten minutes or so earlier than usual, and if possible to find a quiet corner that will then provide a space for your own prayer before the service starts and everyone else arrives.

- *The Lord's Prayer.* When the disciples asked Jesus how to pray, he gave them the prayer we call the Lord's Prayer. It is a prayer that encompasses the whole of life – in heaven and on earth, our need of forgiveness and our reliance upon God – and it can be prayed wherever we are. The traditional prayers of our spiritual and faith heritage are perhaps the ones we will remember in times of need; and, along with a well-remembered favourite prayer, they are the ones that can be prayed quietly, from the heart, when the days are busy.

- *Motto.* This is one to think and pray through before reaching the motorway! A 'motto' is a word or short phrase that speaks to you about you and God, and it is a word or phrase that when used can bring to us a sense of the presence and peace of God.

  In the Bible one of the themes that runs throughout is that of our being called by God, and called by our name: 'I have called you by name' (Isaiah 43.1), the God who is 'acquainted with all my ways', as the psalmist writes (139.3). So the word or phrase that is chosen speaks and expresses something of our identity with and to God, of our faith, and of our own personal relationship with the God who calls to us. Ignatius of Loyola's 'motto' became the motto used by the Jesuits: 'For the greater glory of God'.

When we looked at 'Sacred space and sacred place' (Chapter 6), it was said that by holding in the mind and the imagination a special place which becomes transformed into a sacred space through our encounter there with God, then it could help to bring about an inner quietness and stillness before a time of prayer. In a similar way, discovering our own personal 'motto' can also become a way of our reaching out to God, especially when the days are busy, and so to experience and to be held even for the briefest of moments in the stillness and the peace of God.

Think of five or six favourite verses or phrases from the Bible, from hymns or poems, and write then down. Then gradually and prayerfully begin to discard them one at a time until only one is left, and use this as your 'motto' prayer. Another way would be to take a word from each of the verses chosen and bring them together to form a short phrase, which then becomes your own personal prayer. Chosen prayerfully, the 'motto' will be a prayer that speaks from the very depths of who you are, and of your relationship with God; and so when it is used and spoken, it will bring with it an awareness of God with you, and the Spirit dwelling within.

The word or phrase that has been chosen may not be one that accompanies us along the whole journey of our Pathway to God. As we change through the different experiences and encounters in life, so too the 'motto' which is right for us this week, month or year, may not be quite as right for us the following week, month or year. It may also be that you discover over time more than one 'motto' that can provide for you a depth of meaning, into which you can reach and so come to know God with you.

To discover your own personal 'motto', then, it may be helpful to pray this through when life is travelling along the normal Pathway, and not going at speed down the fast lane of the motorway! Although, of course, even then we may be surprised at what can be God-breathed into our thoughts and hearts, as a word or phrase rises to the surface of our minds in the midst of all of our activity; this will remind us again that we are not travelling the Pathway alone.

- *Music.* The same can apply to music. Listening to music is also prayer, and so playing a piece of music (that again speaks of God to you) in the car can be another way of praying when life seems to leave the Pathway and heads off along the motorway instead. If the music you have chosen is a hymn or a song with words, then sing along; when you sing you also pray, and according to Augustine, to sing is to pray twice!

These suggestions of 'busy time' prayers are of course prayers that can be prayed at any time – when we have the space and the quietness, and when life is hectic and difficult.

Pause for prayer

The Lord is my pace setter, I shall not rush,
He makes me stop and rest for quiet intervals,
He provides me with images of stillness, which restore my serenity.
He leads me in the ways of efficiency; through calmness of mind,
And his guidance is peace.
Even though I have a great many things to accomplish each day,
I will not fret for his presence is here.
His timelessness, his all-importance will keep me in balance.
He prepares refreshment and renewal in the midst of my activity
By anointing my mind with his oils of tranquillity,
My cup of joyous energy overflows.
Surely harmony and effectiveness shall be the fruits of my hours,
For I shall walk in the pace of my Lord, and dwell in his house for ever.

(Toki Miyashina, based on Psalm 23)

13

An oasis: slowing down on retreats and quiet days

We cannot live through life at a continuous and seemingly unending fast pace without taking adequate rest and giving to ourselves the space to be renewed, in body, mind and soul. From the fast lane of the motorway we now come to change down a gear or two as our journey takes us down the sliproad to find an oasis to sit beside – which will hopefully be a place of welcome, a place of stillness, providing a space for you, yourself.

The oasis we have arrived at is a quiet day, which may be half a day, an evening or a full day. You may have experienced a quiet day, or have been away for a few days or more, to stay at a retreat house to be guided through a time of silence, prayer and rest. Here we will look at quiet days, but all that is said of a quiet day relates also to a longer retreat – both invite the one 'retreating from the world' to be met by, and to encounter God; to be treated by the God who loves us.

- *How easy is it to take the time to go on a quiet day, or for a longer retreat?*
- *Is this a part of your own spiritual and prayer life? If it is, what do you enjoy most from the day?*
- *If you haven't experienced a quiet day or retreat, would you like to, and what do you think a quiet day is?*

Rest, relaxation and discipline are important . . . Many people do not know how to rest. They are like rolling locomotives, fuelled by anguish, and perhaps by the fear of stopping. And when they do stop, it is just to sleep more, or to potter around, not knowing what to do. Each one of us must find our own secret rhythm of how to rest, relax and find re-creation, for each one of us is different. We need personal space and time . . . we must discover how to harmonise the active and the passive in us.

(Jean Vanier, The Broken Body)

We may not achieve all of this on one quiet day, but just as Jesus often went somewhere quiet to get away from the crowds, spending time on a quiet day can begin to set in place within us a deeper awareness of our need for our own personal space for reflection, rest and relaxation, and so we begin to learn how to bring a sense of harmony to our lives. Jesus went to his place of retreat and renewal, to sit in silence and prayer, knowing that, as he did, God was present with him.

That God is present is also the hope and expectation of those leading and those participating in a quiet day! Yet it is for each person to decide how close they wish to be with God at that time, how deep within themselves they will let their prayer take them; God is present with us, waiting for and desiring us to move closer into that presence with both patience and love.

What is a quiet day?

- *It is a retreat away from the world and the busy-ness of our usual day* – to step outside the usual routine of life for as many hours as the quiet day lasts. A quiet day can be hard work! You may feel that all you have done is to sit, to ponder and pray; but it is surprising how tired you may feel at the end of the day, as physically and mentally the body enjoys this 'time off' from its usual daily routine, allowing the spiritual within us to come to the surface. At the same time, the peacefulness that surrounds a quiet day brings with it an element of rest and relaxation that may only be fully realized once home again.

- *It is to enter into a time of silence* – which may be welcomed or approached with trepidation. One of the greatest concerns and challenges some seem to have about retreats and quiet days, is the silence; yet the silence is rarely silent, as surrounding sounds can be heard as much as our own heartbeat. The silence, in between the reflections which are offered, may last from 20 minutes to over an hour. A space is then provided for inner stillness, and away from any conversation that may interrupt our silent and spiritual conversation with God.

  The more quiet days we have experienced, then the longer the period of silence will be that we can cope with. Usually the silence is never left 'empty', as prayer suggestions will be offered, and there may be handouts with poems, pictures, prayers or reflections to help focus the mind to prayer and quietness in the silence.

- *How much value do you place on silence?*
- *If you find time to be silent in prayer, how comfortable does that silence then feel?*

  We should never be afraid of entering into silence as we come to pray.

- *Are you afraid of silence?*
- *Is that a fear of encountering God, or of journeying deeper within to discover something more of the truth of who you are?*

Time in silence and in prayer can be and should be life giving, as we spend this very special time with the God of our creation, 'in whom we live and move and have our being' (Acts 17.8). We may be surprised at what we discover and feel is being revealed to us in the silence of our prayer, how God may touch our inner being, even if we are hesitant or reluctant to encounter God and our selves at this depth of inner stillness. Once we discover a depth of silence within us and around us, we may also discover the paradox of a silence that is both noisy and quiet, still and calm, vibrant and full of energy; hopefully also alive with the presence of God.

- Hopefully it will be *to discover a 'sacred space' for yourself* – there is the physical space where the quiet day is being held which leads to seeking the inner space in which to become still and to encounter God. It creates the space in which to pray, and perhaps to pray in ways that may be new – for example: to paint or draw; using clay; to write your own poetry or prose; using images of creation; or one of the ways we have already looked at within this book.

- There is *the potential of discovering something more about who we are* – when we are provided with the space and the time to pray, away from everyone else who usually shares our days, giving to us the time to think about issues that are important, particular concerns or any decisions that need to be made. Being on a quiet day can enable us to become more open to the presence of God, which can then become for us a time of discernment about our own calling in life and in faith, a time of personal spiritual 'indulgence', rest and relaxation; and, as Jean Vanier writes, to discover how to harmonize the active and the passive.

- Quiet days are rarely, if ever, held for one person on his or her own and so they will be *a gathering of people* whom you may know, perhaps some well and others not so well, or you may never have met them before. This means that it is important to remember that each person on the quiet day will have come from his or her own particular Pathway; and each will bring their own personal journey experiences of life, their own way of praying, their own image of God, their own problems and dreams.

- *It can be challenging*, and may bring to the surface a certain vulnerability as we come before God, as we encounter the silence offered. Initially, just to arrive at the venue may bring a sense of vulnerability as each person comes, perhaps unsure of what the day may hold, or if they will be asked to do something. As the quiet day progresses, the vulnerability may come through the times of prayer, of silence, and the possibility of hearing God speak into our hearts, of discovering a new direction in life, a new calling, or coming to experience something new of the love of God.

If participation within the group is a part of the day, for example sharing something of their own thoughts from their own prayer, then it is up to each person to decide whether to join in and how comfortable they are with sharing with others present. Within the day, though, through the reflections and the times of silence, participation is personal and individual; one to one with God.

For those partaking, the hope would be that, discovered beneath and beyond all the busy-ness of each day – all the pressures, stresses, worries, burdens, all of the mundane calls upon our time, all the things that have to be planned and organized – there is a sacred space and place of stillness where we can reconnect with the deepest longings lying within us, with God and with our self, and so come to discover or rediscover all that God calls us to be, maybe a re-knowing of who we are.

The quiet day offers to each person present space and stillness, and, prompted by the reflections given, to sift through the multitude of thoughts, concerns, decisions to be made that lie within, and hopefully to find the right Pathway to walk on.

An oasis

It is an opportunity to take time out to rest so that our energies are restored; and what may be needed is to find a comfortable chair to curl up in and then go to sleep! It is to pray our own prayers, or spend time reading the prayerful thoughts of someone else. It is to come to be at peace with ourselves once more. Most importantly, it is to be our self and allow the Spirit of God to meet with us, and then to take from the day whatever we feel is right.

John O'Donohue in his book *Eternal Echoes* writes:

> In the silence of our prayer we should be able to sense the roguish smile of a joyful God who, despite all the chaos and imperfection, ultimately shelters everything . . . Beneath your actions, gestures and thoughts there is a silent tranquillity . . . a pure place of unity which the noise of life can never disturb . . . In stillness, the silence of the Divine becomes intimate.

In the quietness of a quiet day, we can, if we desire, meet with the God who holds us and dwells within, and so find the richness of the pool of tranquillity where we are totally at one with God, and so come to know the peace that will enable us to re-encounter the noise and busy-ness of the world once more.

Pause for prayer

Our own personal Pathway to God: our faith journey

The Pathway to God is unique to each one of us. It is a Pathway that has been, and still is, being shaped by all that we experience, personally, as we journey through life. To look at the Pathway that has been travelled so far can reveal many surprises, bringing to mind memories perhaps thought to be forgotten, and a deeper awareness of how God has been active and present in life.

In whatever way is most helpful, become still and quiet before God.

On a piece of paper, draw two lines to represent a Pathway. Decide where the starting point will be: your earliest memory as a child; a specific number of years ago, for example beginning ten years ago. Then slowly and in the quietness of prayer begin to place 'signposts' on the Pathway which speak to you of significant moments in your life. For example:

- Special events and occasions – happy or sad.
- Achievements.
- Moments of joy.
- Moments of sorrow.
- Times when God has felt very close.
- Times when God has felt far away.
- Times of despair.
- Sense of being alone.
- Decisions made – changes of direction in life.

If you are creative, use colours to express the different 'signposts', or draw onto the Pathway 'road' images to help you map your journey – potholes, bridges, crossroads, traffic lights, roadworks, open limit signs – giving the green light to the imagination!

Take time to look prayerfully at the Pathway which is, in part, your own personal journey map.

Note the pattern of the signposts: of the special events that you have remembered, any times of sorrow and difficulty, and the footsteps of God on the Pathway.

Bring all of this to God in a time of prayer, asking for help in looking at the journey that has been travelled so far, to accept that journey, to offer a prayer of thanksgiving for all that has been encountered and has shaped your life, and to have the faith to look ahead with joy and hope.

Ask God to be with you on the Pathway that still awaits to be travelled.

Spend a little time to reflect on this time of prayer.

14

How far along the Pathway to God has our journey taken us?

How much has been discovered on the Pathway about the different ways of praying that bring us closer to God and to understanding ourselves? How much has been discovered, so far, about all that makes you, you?

Following the way in prayer means that as we pray and seek out a deeper relationship with God, then we come to meet with, and touch, the spiritual within us. Prayer is probably easier to define and describe than spirituality is. Prayer can be simply described as being our communication and relationship with God, and God's with us. Spirituality is a word that includes all that we can say about prayer, but at the same time it also needs a broader definition and understanding, which takes in the whole of our lives and how we live out our lives in faith. It is also a much-used word throughout all areas of society, within religious and non-religious contexts.

A part of the spiritual involves knowing who we are as a person; that continuous journey of discovering all that makes us 'tick' – our likes and dislikes, our strengths and weaknesses. Added to this is the way in which we are able, or not, to bring the whole of our selves before God in prayer. The spiritual dimension of 'who we are as a person' is not confined to our times of prayer or being in a church service – our faith and our relationship with God has to reach out beyond our inner self, to include the rest of the world.

The prayers we have travelled with through this book are ones that concentrate on our own very personal journey to a deeper awareness and understanding of our life of faith. Yet, at the same time, they are offered in a way that enables us, as we come to know ourselves better, to become more aware of the wider concerns of the world. Spirituality can never be easily defined, and in a group of people there will probably be a variety of ideas and explanations; but a simple definition of spirituality could be: 'A living out from the felt experiences of God in a way that enables and brings about a wholeness of being, that can then reach out to embrace the world.'

If our spirituality is our lived-out experience of God in our lives, then the way we live this out will be shaped by the person we are – our past and present experiences and encounters in life, and all of our future hopes and dreams. It will also be shaped by our journey of faith and the Pathway we walk on, and helped by the unfolding understanding of all that our faith means to us, all that we learn and discover through belonging to a church community, through reading our Bible, through prayer, and through being with others with whom we can share something of our journey and listen to theirs as well.

The spiritual tradition of the Jesuits and the heritage of Ignatius of Loyola have had a big impact on my life, helping me to discover and understand who I am, and how I see and know myself, and God. Reading about the life and ministry of Cuthbert (643–89), the Bishop of Lindisfarne, has provided inspiration, as has something of the silence that comes with the Benedictine way. This is the mix of spiritual traditions which feeds my life of prayer and faith.

Many may never come to name a particular spiritual tradition that reaches into their lives and lives of prayer, but recognize that a particular way of praying is the way in which God is known and felt. It is, perhaps, more important or at least more relevant to begin with, to find a way of praying that we are comfortable with, and challenged by: a way of praying in which we sense and know God with us.

Spirituality, within the Christian context, is about relationship and discipleship, and so it encompasses the whole of our life journey, of our self with our self, with other people, with the rest of the world, and with God. As we grow and mature – in age as much as in faith – then the way we express our relationship with God will also, hopefully, grow and mature.

Spirituality can also be seen as being a movement of the Spirit within us that moves to the beat and the rhythm of our lives. It is to hear the call of Jesus to follow him in faith, and the God who is with us always, encouraging and challenging us, not asking anything of us that we cannot give or do, yet knowing what our potential is and wanting us to know it as well.

Spirituality is a call to let God be God in our lives, and for us to be rooted and grounded in God, to seek a deeper relationship with God, and so come to know a deeper meaning and purpose in life; and it is to know God in the everydayness of our lives as well as in those special moments.

Spirituality calls for a uniting of the whole of our selves, body, mind and spirit, to be holistic; and this raises a number of questions to think and pray over:

- *Who am I?*
- *Who is God to me?*
- *Where and how do I feel and know God's love/peace/presence?*
- *What brings me to a deeper awareness of God?*
- *How do I pray and meet with God in prayer?*
- *How do I bring the God within, out into the wider world?*
- *How does my prayer and my faith affect the way in which I respond to the world in which I live?*

Pause for prayer

Looking back to look forward

The spiritual life, the life of the people of God, is portrayed throughout the Bible as being a journey, and so our own life in faith, being a journey, is one of movement: a movement that looks and points to the future. It is good, though, on that journey to stop and pause, to journey within, to look at the Pathway already walked, and to look ahead to where that Pathway may lead us.

Whenever we begin a journey, then the aim is usually to reach a particular destination – the starting point is A, and we keep our eyes on the finishing line until we come to B. Our journey of faith begins at our baptism, gathers momentum as we discover for ourselves the love of God and make a commitment to follow the way of Jesus, and then it takes a varying route depending upon how we are called to be a disciple in the world. Our destination, though, is the same regardless of the journey: the eternal life promised to us, as Paul writes to the church at Philippi, 'I press on towards the goal for the prize of the heavenly call of God in Christ Jesus' (Philippians 3.14).

Our eyes may be fixed firmly ahead, yet how often do we stop and look backwards at the path we have already travelled? If we seek the way of God then we need to look backwards, to reflect over the past, in a way that will help us travel more lightly and confidently into the future. All that we have encountered and experienced has an impact on the person we are, the way we view God, the way we live out our lives.

By looking backwards we can come to discover the continual touch of God, and how we have felt or realized that touch over the years, in our day-to-day lives – the special moments when God has felt particularly close, or far away. We can also discover how we have grown in faith and how we have dealt with the painful and difficult situations that life throws at us. There may be times when prayerful looking back is needed to enable us to look more clearly at a particular issue; and to do this, another person, a trusted friend or spiritual director or companion, could help to unravel all that lies deep within.

To move from the specific to the more general, this 'looking back' within Ignatian spirituality is called the Examen; or, to give it its full – and slightly off-putting – name, Examination of Consciousness! Reading the book *Eternal Echoes* by John O'Donohue, philosopher and spirituality writer in the Celtic tradition, I came across these words: 'It is valuable practice at night to spend a little while revisiting the invisible sanctuaries of your lived day. Each day is a secret story woven around the radiant heart of wonder.'

To revisit the sanctuaries of the day is what 'looking back to look forward' is all about, to revisit in prayer the sanctuaries of the day just gone, or the week or the month or the year. Imagine watching a video of the day you have had; and, to try to see how and where God has been present or not, look at how you have reacted and responded to all that has been experienced in that day. Then pick out one special moment to give thanks for. This is a way of praying that can be prayed at any time, but perhaps especially last thing at night, which gives us the opportunity to reflect over the day in preparation for the day to follow, maybe prayed within the short service of Night Prayer or Compline. It is a prayer that can be prayed in ten minutes or longer – take as long as you need.

- Find a quiet time to yourself, with space to sit and be with God. Spend a short while to become still and quiet within, to empty the mind of the busy-ness of the day, and become aware of any sounds around – breathing, traffic, clocks – let them go. Place yourself, as far as you are comfortable with, into the presence of God.

- Begin with a prayer of thanksgiving, with the awareness that all you have and are comes as a gift from God.

- Picture before God the day you have had – the places you have been to, people met, conversations, all you have done and not done. It's not necessary to recall every single moment! Be neutral and non-judging, but note what has happened, and any significant or unexpected moments.

- Think through how you felt – any feelings of sorrow or joy, being full of energy or drained – and note where you felt the presence of God in the day, and where you didn't feel the presence of God.

- Speak to God as one friend to another. Ask forgiveness where needed, but do so with a gentleness on yourself, remembering that you are loved and cherished by God.

- Then give thanks for the day, and in particular give thanks for one very special moment of that day. Within the prayer, listen also to God and hear God thank you for the time spent together.

- End the time of prayer by looking in hope towards the day to come, and ask God to be with you in that new day and all that it may ask of you.

15

An ending or a beginning?

———⇒•◦•⇐———

The path before, behind, seen.
Yet, how far has been travelled
Through stillness and silence,
Through music and transforming creativity
Of prayer that is God-breathed,
Spirit-met in the depths
Of our being?

Whenever we read a book, eventually we arrive at the last page, the last paragraph, the last full stop; and so we reach the end. Here in this book we are about to journey towards its closing thoughts and make our way to the last full stop of this prayerful Pathway to God. Have we reached an ending or a beginning?

Prayer is with us always, and is unceasing, never-ending, as the God we pray to is present with us always, eternally Emmanuel. So hopefully this is not really the end, but just a time to pause on the journey to take another look at the prayers that have been prayed, familiar ones or new ones, and those that are still to be prayed, so that we can continue along the Pathway of faith with those prayers, and with all that has been revealed to us.

As the Pathway of prayer continues to interweave itself more and more into all of our days, then more will be discovered of the variety of prayers that bind us in relationship to God and creation, the prayers that open up our deepest feelings, the prayers through which we are touched and enlivened by the Spirit.

An ending or a beginning?

Pause for prayer

I pray that the God of our Lord Jesus Christ,
the Father of glory,
may give you a spirit of wisdom and revelation as you come to know him,
so that,
with the eyes of your heart enlightened,
you may know what is the hope to which he has called you,
what are the riches of his glorious inheritance among the saints,
and what is the immeasurable greatness of his power for us who believe,
according to the working of his great power.

I pray that, according to the riches of his glory,
he may grant that you may be strengthened in your inner being
with power through his Spirit,
and that Christ may dwell in your hearts through faith,
as you are being rooted and grounded in love.
I pray that you may have the power to comprehend,
with all the saints,
what is the breadth and length and height and depth,
and to know the love of Christ that surpasses knowledge,
so that you may be filled with all the fullness of God.

(Ephesians 1.17–19 and 3.16–19)

References

All Bible quotes and references are taken from the New Revised Standard Version.

Common Worship: Services and Prayers for the Church of England (Church House Publishing, 2000).

Herbert, George, *The Country Parson, The Temple* (Paulist Press, 1981).

Miyashina, Toki, 'The Lord is my pace setter', from *The SPCK Book of Christian Prayer* (SPCK, 1997).

O'Donohue, John, *Anam Cara* (Bantam Books, 1999).

O'Donohue, John, *Divine Beauty* (Bantam Books, 2004).

O'Donohue, John, *Eternal Echoes* (Bantam Books, 2000).

Sheldrake, Philip, *Spaces for the Sacred* (SCM Press, 2001).

Shepherd, Richard, 'Music in these stones', in S. Platten and C. Lewis (eds), *Flagships of the Spirit: Cathedrals in Society* (Darton, Longman and Todd, 1998).

Vanier, Jean, *The Broken Body* (Darton, Longman and Todd, 2003).

The Society for Promoting Christian Knowledge (SPCK) was founded in 1698. Its mission statement is:

To promote Christian knowledge by
- **Communicating the Christian faith in its rich diversity;**
- **Helping people to understand the Christian faith and to develop their personal faith; and**
- **Equipping Christians for mission and ministry.**

SPCK Worldwide serves the Church through Christian literature and communication projects in over 100 countries, and provides books for those training for ministry in many parts of the developing world. This worldwide service depends upon the generosity of others and all gifts are spent wholly on ministry programmes, without deductions.

SPCK Bookshops support the life of the Christian community by making available a full range of Christian literature and other resources, providing support for those training for ministry, and assisting bookstalls and book agents throughout the UK.

SPCK Publishing produces Christian books and resources, covering a wide range of inspirational, pastoral, practical and academic subjects. Authors are drawn from many different Christian traditions, and publications aim to meet the needs of a wide variety of readers in the UK and throughout the world.

The Society does not necessarily endorse the individual views contained in its publications, but hopes they stimulate readers to think about and further develop their Christian faith.

For further information about the Society, visit our website at *www.spck.org.uk* or write to:
SPCK, 36 Causton Street,
London SW1P 4ST, United Kingdom.